ADIRONDACK STYLE

Look to yourselves, ye polished gentlemen!
No city airs or arts pass current here.
Your rank is all reversed; let men of cloth
Bow to the stalwart churls in overalls:
They are the doctors of the wilderness,
And we the low-prized laymen.
In sooth, red flannel is a saucy test
Which few can put on with impunity.
What make you, master, fumbling at the oar?
Will you catch crabs? Truth tries pretention here.
The sallow knows the basket-makers thumb;
The oar, the guide's. Dare you accept the tasks
He shall impose, to find a spring, trap foxes,
Tell the sun's time, determine the true north,
Or stumbling on through vast self-similar woods
To thread by night the nearest way to camp?

RALPH WALDO EMERSON —from *The Adirondacs*

ADIRONDACK STYLE

Ann Stillman O'Leary

Photographs by Gary R. Hall

Introduction by Elizabeth Folwell

Editor, *Adirondack Life* magazine

Clarkson Potter / Publishers
New York

To Bill, whose patience with me is astounding,

and to my children, Martha and Willy

Published by Clarkson Potter/Publishers, New York, New York. Member of the Crown Publishing Group, a division of Random House, Inc.

www.randomhouse.com

CLARKSON N. POTTER is a trademark and POTTER and colophon are registered trademarks of Random House, Inc.

Originally published in hardcover by Clarkson Potter/ Publishers in 1998.

Printed in China

Library of Congress Cataloging-in-Publication Data

O'Leary, Ann S.
    Adirondack style / Ann S. O'Leary ; photography by Gary R. Hall; introduction by Elizabeth Folwell. — 1st ed.
        p.   cm.
    Includes bibliographical references.
    1. Architecture, Domestic—New York (State)—Adirondack Mountains Region. 2. Interior architecture—New York (State)—Adirondack Mountains Region. 3. Vacation homes—New York (State)—Adirondack Mountains Region. 4. Regionalism in architecture—New York (State)—Adirondack Mountains Region. 5. Camps—New York (State)—Adirondack Mountains Region. 6. Decoration and ornament, Rustic—New York (State)—Adirondack Mountains Region. 7. Adirondack Park (N.Y.) I. Title.
NA7575.O43 1998
728.7'2'097475—dc21   98-9172
                                                                          CIP
ISBN 0-609-80235-6

10 9 8 7 6 5 4 3 2 1

First paperback edition

Developed and produced by Julie Stillman, South Hero, Vermont
Design: Robert A. Yerks and Jill E. Schwenderman
Stylists: Ann Stillman O'Leary, Heidi Roland, Constance Keller

PREFACE

I can date the inception of *Adirondack Style* to the fall of 1989, when I was fortunate enough to visit a home that would be recognized as the watershed for regional architecture in the Great Camp tradition. This new camp by the progressive and internationally acclaimed firm Bohlin Cywinski Jackson had left tradition in the dust and pushed camp design to the brink of modern architecture. In this single interpretation of the Adirondack vernacular I could foresee the exciting and far-reaching implications for its future. Had I set out to write this book in 1989, there would have been only three or four homes to photograph. After a fifty-year hiatus, the revival of this rustic style was as slow-moving as a glacial retreat. In 1997, however, the time was right and, most important, I had a publisher.

My intent here is to examine the origins of the Adirondack Great Camp style and illustrate how it is being interpreted today, in both newly built and renovated camps. I have organized the book according to the exterior and interior design elements that define "camp," so for each category there are examples shown from many different camps. I have chosen to feature two camps (Bissell and Stewart) that embody all of these elements and epitomize Adirondack style.

After logging over 20,000 miles on my car—venturing over remote and rocky roads at impossible inclines, and enduring more climate than I knew existed—I am ready to bid this project a fond farewell and send it out into the world.

It is important to pay tribute to Harvey Kaiser, whose book *Great Camps of the Adirondacks* documented the very existence of these structures and gave them historical significance. His book has become a compendium of information for camp owners and builders alike.

I would like to extend a heartfelt thank you to all of the gracious owners of the exceptional places included in this book. Without these willing subjects there would have been no book. I felt blessed to walk their back forties and was treated like an old acquaintance by many. To respect their privacy, some specific names and locations are not mentioned. I hope they will take as much pride as I do in the words and images presented here.

I am fortunate to have convinced Betsy Folwell, editor of *Adirondack Life* magazine and Adirondack expert extraordinaire, to write the historic overview. Her insights set the stage for what's happening in Adirondack style today. She has been my guide through the back roads of the Adirondacks as well as the thickets of creative writing.

A great debt is owed to the following people who took an interest in my project and through suggestion, research, and invaluable leads helped keep it moving: Julie Stillman my editor and sister; Gary Hall, my talented photographer; Heidi Roland, who provided arbitration, creativity, and humor when needed; Ruth Hancock and the Syracuse China Company; Connie Keller and Hope Frenette, my sisters-in-law, who shared their expertise; interior decorator Barbara Collum; librarian Jerry Pepper and photo researcher Jim Meehan of the Adirondack Museum; twig worker Crispin Shakeshaft and partner Cynthia Floor; Mary Hotaling, Laura Viscome, Robert McLaughlin, Julie Turner, and all of the caretakers who cheerfully came to my aid when needed. I also owe thanks to my father, and to my mother, who I felt provided direction and guidance from the great beyond.

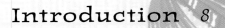

Contents

826 BLUE MOUNTAIN FROM "THE HEDGES" BOAT HOUSE.
BLUE MOUNTAIN LAKE, N. Y...ADIRONDACK MTS.

Rocky Point Inn, Fourth Lake, Adirondack Mts.

COPYRIGHT, 1903, BY DETROIT PHOTOGRAPHIC CO.

THE ADIRONDACKS: FROM INDIANS TO INDUSTRIALISTS

ELIZABETH FOLWELL

Look at any New York road map. Now focus on the northeastern corner of the state, a section bounded by Lake Champlain to the east, the St. Lawrence River to the north, and the Mohawk River to the south. Within that quadrant, zero in a bit more on the jagged shield-shaped outline of the Adirondack Park, an area of some six million acres, a state park far bigger than Yosemite and Yellowstone national parks combined, bigger than the whole state of Connecticut. The word Adirondack is supposed to have its roots in an Algonquin Indian phrase roughly meaning "they eat bark," an insult aimed at their Iroquois enemies, who roamed this rugged terrain. The borders of this curious mix of wilderness and civilization surround some three thousand lakes and

ponds, thousands of miles of free-flowing rivers, and innumerable mountain chains. There are craggy, timberless peaks with snow-swept alpine summits and slopes cloaked with impenetrable tangles of spruce and balsam fir. Hardwood forests of sugar maple, yellow birch, and beech cover rolling hills that glow red, gold, and bronze in the autumn. In remote backwaters, old-growth pine, with trunks so immense that the arms of four grown men could not encircle them, stand tall over ponds that seem untouched by modern times.

Within this park are more than a hundred communities, ranging from world-famous Lake Placid to off-the-beaten-track hamlets like Beaver River (sorry, you can only get to this year-round enclave on Stillwater Reservoir by boat or snowmobile). The park designation dates back to 1892, when laws were passed to preserve the remaining forests and watersheds. The region includes public lands owned by the State of New York (slightly over forty percent) and private holdings that include hundreds of thousands of acres held by multinational timber concerns, immense family estates, and venerable clubs, as well as ordinary homes on village lots. Approximately 130,000 people live in the Adirondack Park, and the annual count for tourists varies greatly depending on who you ask and when you ask them. On a fine day in July, when cars with exotic license plates jam the parking lots of the Adirondack Museum, in Blue Mountain Lake, it seems that six (or eight or nine) million visitors could be a likely figure, but on a sleety day in mud season (April is *not* spring in the North Country, but merely winter's bitter end), it's hard to scare up more than a handful of locals. In many hamlets, deer are more plentiful than people.

The landscape — imagine Vermont's handsome Green Mountains coupled with Maine's clear ponds and streams — was molded by glaciers more than ten thousand years ago. The mile-thick slow-moving ice carved the lakes, scoured their drainage rivers, smoothed the mountaintops, and left behind sinuous eskers of sand shaped like thin, bony spines. Several types of forests now flourish on these hillsides, with hardwoods, softwoods, and alpine shrubs occupying the different zones from the valleys to the summits. The region abounds in wildlife: moose (extirpated in the 1870s, but gradually coming back on their own), mountain lions (officially gone by the 1890s, but still occasionally sighted), whitetail deer, wolf (hunted out thanks to generous bounties), black bear (plentiful), wolverine (trapped out), red fox, gray fox, fisher, mink, otter, ermine, pine marten, snowshoe hare, plus voles, moles, lemmings, mice, shrews, and bats. Above the lakes and trees soar bald eagles, osprey, ravens, peregrine falcons, and other raptors, and in the woods are ruffed and spruce grouse, woodcock, woodpeckers, and songbirds of all stripes. The waters harbor ducks, loons, geese, herons, and kingfishers, along with brook trout, lake trout, landlocked salmon, bass, pickerel, whitefish, and the ubiquitous beaver.

The region's human history began with Ice Age hunters. The first Native visitors probably looked upon the region as a prime source of furs, food, materials for baskets (such as sweetgrass, ash splints, and bark), and herbs and roots for medicine. In fair weather, these people ventured from temperate river valleys to camp along the shores of Lake George, Long Lake, Tupper Lake, Cranberry Lake, and countless interior rivers. They built their seasonal homes of supple branches lashed together and sheathed with sheets of bark, and used the abundant hard glacial stones for campfire rings. This migration continued for generations.

Map of New York State with the Adirondack Park outlined in the northeast corner.

"I stood for the first time on the cool, mossy shore of the mountain springlet lake, Tear-of-the-clouds. ...This lovely pool lifted on its granite pedestal toward heaven, the loftiest water mirror of the stars; beseeching... from each low drifting cloud some tribute for the sources of the Hudson; fresh, new, and un-visited, save by wild beasts that drank; it was a gem more pure and more delightful to the eye than the most precious jewel."

— Verplanck Colvin, circa 1870 Superintendent for the State of New York Adirondack Survey.

In 1609, two explorers spied the Adirondack region from afar: Samuel de Champlain glided down the lake that now bears his name in the company of Algonquin scouts, and landed near Ticonderoga, a fertile, protected plain that was home to Iroquois families. To make a long story short, Champlain blasted three Iroquois with his arquebus shortly after getting out of his boat, beginning a conflict over control of the land that lasted for 150 years. Just a few months after Champlain's fateful foray, which assured that the Iroquois would distrust and despise the French, Henry Hudson sailed up the river that now bears *his* name. Whether he spotted the blue-gray hills to the north or not, Hudson suspected that there were riches to be found on the shores just off his anchorage.

While power, wealth, and the greater glory of their respective kings motivated these two men, the next Europeans who arrived in the Adirondack wilderness were driven by style. Furs — especially fur hats — were the pinnacle of fashion in England and on the Continent, and beaver (the key fiber in high-quality felt), fisher (akin to sable in its sheen and texture), ermine, otter, marten, and wolverine all grew thick, lustrous pelts in the long, cold winters. As early as 1611 there was a fur factory at Montreal, and French traders traveled the length of Lake Champlain; when the Dutch established a fort near Albany a few decades later, their men went up the Mohawk River and over from the Hudson to find furs.

Initially Native Americans supplied raw pelts, but it was only a matter of time before white trappers penetrated the deep woods that grew beyond the flat river valleys and

▲ *The Battle of Ticonderoga, 1609. The legend reads: "A. The Iroquois fort. [Letter missing in illustration.] B. The enemy. C. The enemy canoes of oak-bark, each holding 10, 15, or 18 men. D, E. Two chiefs killed, one wounded by an arquebus-shot of Sieur de Champlain. F. The Sieur de Champlain. G. Two arquebusiers of Sieur de Champlain. [Letter missing] H. Montagnais, Hurons, and Algonquins. [Letter misplaced.] I. Birch-bark canoes of our savage allies. K. Woods. [Letter missing.]"*
(Courtesy of Cornell University Library, Ithaca, New York)

found their own supply. Numerous big rivers that flowed from the high mountains provided the best means to reach more furs in the wild and products of far-flung Indian camps. This casual trade and sporadic reconnaissance continued for more than a century, and shiploads of skins made fortunes for many.

While we may like to imagine the Adirondacks as a place removed from the whims and worries of the rest of the world, that notion was as false 260 years ago as it is today. In 1734, eager to lay claim to a potential empire south of the St. Lawrence, the French constructed a massive fort at Crown Point, a vantage point on Lake Champlain that offered clear lines of sight for miles in many directions. Some forty miles to the south, the English were in control, so the French stronghold was no hastily thrown-together stockade, but a four-story octagonal chateau with twelve-foot-thick walls — a state-of-the-art marvel of military architecture. Among the French forces were skilled masons, carpenters, and blacksmiths to shape rooms and forge hardware, along with farmers, herdsmen, and their families to supply food for the troops (although the soldiers no doubt hunted and fished in the trackless woods beyond the fort). Crown Point, however briefly, was a self-sufficient French community on the fringe of deep wilderness.

The French and Indian War erupted in 1755, and the strategically placed fort was key to controlling an immense water highway that connected British and French territories. After many attacks, the British and American forces finally captured Crown Point in 1759, and a period of relative stability ensued. Some settlers, such as Irishman William Gilliland, moved to Champlain's western shores to found a string of sturdy agricultural towns; a few more moved into the Mohawk Valley, including William Johnson, who set up a huge English-style estate on the Mohawk River complete with slaves and indentured servants. Gilliland and Johnson both were intimately aware of timber and other resources just beyond their settlements, but war broke out, this time between the upstart colonials and the British.

The Adirondack perimeter to the east and south was once again a battle zone, and soldiers made temporary homes in the muddy shadows of the French and Indian War forts at Ticonderoga and Crown Point. The enlisted men lived in huts made of branches, brush, and bark, or covered their cloth tents with bark sheets to keep out the weather. Officers had frame houses, with hewn timbers and shingle roofs supplied by a corps of engineers and builders. Conditions, especially for enlisted men, were truly wretched: winter cold and snow were unrelenting; spring brought clouds of biting insects; and there was never enough to eat or drink at any time of year. Eyewitness accounts speak of soldiers drowning as they slept in their hovels. Once the war was over, land in the Adirondacks was offered as mustering-out pay, with acreage determined by rank; precious few availed themselves of this dubious opportunity.

Following the American Revolution, land speculators snatched up millions of Adirondack acres at very little cost; these tracts were divided and subdivided, sight unseen, until the end of the eighteenth century. According to William Reed, who wrote a charming reminiscence about the 1820s called *Life on the Border*, the North Country became a "center of attraction for poor men because of the cheapness of the land. ... A few brought teams and a little household furniture, but very rarely one brought money enough to pay for his own land. ... We plunged into the forest, adopted the rude life of frontier people ... and set about organizing a home in the wilderness."

By the early 1830s, many young families from Massachusetts, Vermont, New Hampshire, and French Canada had moved into the Adirondacks. Settlers gravitated toward easily accessible lakes, or rivers where water would power the saw- and gristmills essential to creating agricultural communities. In places like North Elba, Port Henry, Old Forge, and Adirondac, they found iron ore so rich that they could pluck it from the hillsides rather than dig pits or mines. From one end of the Adirondacks to the other the timber was superb: pine, spruce, and fir for lumber; hemlock for tanbark; and hardwoods for charcoal to feed the insatiable iron forges. As the rest of New York and the nation grew, local lumber — floated to market on swift rivers — was used to build homes and stores far away from the mountains.

When the Civil War began, there were temporary logging camps in remote forest clearings; prosperous towns in the Champlain Valley; and a few dozen widely scattered hamlets in the heart of the Adirondacks, where families raised sheep for wool (to knit into endless mittens and sweaters), cattle for milk and meat, hogs, chickens, and oats, wheat, corn, potatoes and other vegetables. Even in Hamilton County, which has only a hundred frost-free days a year, they grew tobacco. Folks clustered in modest towns with stores, schools, and churches, living in foursquare homes made of proper lumber, instead of rough log cabins. These early houses drew on the styles of the pioneers' homelands: steep roofs from Quebec, welcoming front porches from New England, and created communities that look like they had been built to last, regardless of the deep wilderness that lay just beyond the last cleared field.

The untamed woods and waters were looked upon as a source of fuel, furs for cash and clothing, wild meat, berries, building material, and even sweetener, in the form of maple sugar. Although settlements were isolated — in many cases the only reliable transportation was by boat — residents were very aware of the great urban centers to the south and the booming industrial towns a day's travel from the edge of the woods. As early as the 1840s, a few city "sports" began coming to the Adirondacks to hunt and fish in the summers, but it took a book written by a Boston preacher to turn those intrepid few into an army.

William H. H. Murray's *Adventures in the Wilderness*, which first appeared as a series of articles in a Connecticut newspaper in 1867, hit the nation's bookshops in 1869 and created a sensation. This collection on hunting, fishing, and tramping the woods was complemented by advice on what to pack, how to reach various destinations, how to hire a guide, and other useful nuggets sandwiched among glowing praise extolling a little-known destination. The Adirondack region was paradise, the preacher proclaimed, a land of incomparable beauty that could be experienced without arduous toil — a place that, by the way, also promised good health. The air itself was good for a body, scented with sweet balsam and packed with salubrious ozone. Murray unequivocally stated "No portion of our country surpasses, if indeed any equals, in health-giving qualities, the Adirondack Wilderness" and went so far as to suggest that ladies might enjoy the woods: "There is nothing in the trip which the most delicate and fragile need fear."

In 1857, William James Stillman sketched Ralph Waldo Emerson, James Russell Lowell, Louis Agassiz, and others on their first Adirondack trip. The next summer the group ventured to Follensby Pond — an event now known as the Philosophers' Camp. (Courtesy of the Concord Free Public Library, Concord, Mass.)

CAMP OF THE ADIRONDAC CLUB . FOLLANSBEE LAKE . 1857.
PAINTED BY W. J. STILLMAN.
BEQUEATHED TO THE LIBRARY BY E. R. HOAR.

Murray's book captivated an audience that was just beginning to embrace the outdoors; only a generation before, the woods and waters were seen as places to be endured or conquered, not enjoyed for their own intrinsic values. Newspapers and magazines started to publish columns by outdoor correspondents that entertained readers with tales of expeditions to unknown territories. As Brendan Gill wrote in a 1978 *New Yorker* essay, "In a mere handful of generations, people went from fearing solitude to seeking it; having built cities so crowded and uncomfortable and disease-ridden as those they had left behind in Europe, they cast about for a means of escaping them. And so the first summer places came into existence."

Spas and hot springs from Arkansas to upstate New York were popular, if passive, ways to enjoy days and weeks away from home. The seashore from North Carolina to Maine attracted summer colonists seeking to escape the relentless city heat. A movement called Muscular Christianity had caught on in Europe and America; its tenets were that exercise and recreation were worthwhile pursuits and that the outdoors was a wonderful part of God's creation, not a sinister force to be subdued. These places and notions appealed to a growing middle class that had something new: leisure time. Hunting and fishing for sport, rather than subsistence, became fashionable, and *Adventures in the Wilderness* became the guide for this population, suggesting new and different places to go.

As Murray's book went through countless editions, Adirondackers adapted to the needs and interests of the new visitors. Along waterways, especially Tupper, Long, Blue Mountain, and Raquette lakes, and the Saranac and Fulton chains of lakes, farmhouse owners added a room, a straw-stuffed mattress, and another chair at the table, and proclaimed their homes inns. Farmers and loggers guided sports through the woods when their own seasonal work was at low ebb. Within a decade of the publication of *Adventures in the Wilderness*, actual hotels with private chambers and the expected amenities were constructed in the woods, and a class of men who described themselves as professional guides had evolved. By the 1870s, rail lines extended into the Adirondack interior as far as North Creek. From there tourists could take stagecoaches and steamboats to Blue Mountain Lake, Raquette Lake, and Long Lake — places that had formerly required many long days of rough travel on primitive trails. Tracks also followed the pastoral valleys of Lake George and Lake Champlain, so that the eastern Adirondacks were also accessible by a combination of trains, coaches, and private buckboard wagons.

By the mid-1880s, full-blown resorts in the Adirondacks rivaled the celebrated watering holes of Newport and Saratoga Springs. These brand-new accommodations boasted string quartets, post offices, barber shops, and newsstands that sold major papers that were only a day or two late. Their chefs prepared seven-course meals, and waiters laid out all the proper silver and poured wine into the correct glasses. Paul Smith's Hotel, on St. Regis Lake, had its own telegraph office, where wealthy guests could stay abreast of world affairs; the Prospect House, on Blue Mountain Lake, had an electric light in every guest room — the first hotel on the face of the earth to have such modern amenities.

Initially, the sheer difficulty of the trip had made the Adirondacks an exclusive place. But the wealthiest visitors were less enthralled when the region became more accessible, and many more guests began arriving at their favorite lodgings. Acquiring property — still a bargain when compared to farmland in the Hudson Valley — and building second homes became the thing to do. These places had to be different, though, than the cottages of Newport and the beach houses of Cape May, where society still dictated certain standards of restraint in recreation, dress, and architecture.

From this privileged class of visitors emerged William West Durant, son of a railroad tycoon and the first Adirondack developer. As a young man, he had studied abroad and developed certain notions of taste and building styles that proved to be quite suitable to the enthusiastic wanna-be Adirondack home owners. Durant took over his father's Adirondack rail line and cast about for more ways to make money. His first real estate project in the late 1870s, Camp Pine Knot, was a collection of simple buildings

➤ *Paul Smith's Hotel, photographed by Seneca Ray Stoddard, one of the well-known Adirondack chroniclers.*
(Courtesy of Paul Smith's College Library, Paul Smiths, New York)

on Raquette Lake's Long Point. There were several sleeping cottages, a two-story main lodge, a dining pavilion, and even a barge that could be anchored out in the lake — promising a restful night a safe distance away from hordes of late-spring blackflies. Inside, the locally made furniture reflected the woods: kneehole desks made of bark and twig, foursquare bedsteads made of logs, and tables topped with burls. The whole ensemble was a planned community, an architectural composition that recalled the Swiss chalet, yet heralded a bold new step. (Later Durant admitted that his inspiration for Camp Pine Knot was the crude hut of an ill-tempered guide named Alvah Dunning. The concept of individual buildings for separate purposes was also common at logging camps of the time, so that, for instance, a fire in the cook shed would not spread quickly to the lumberjacks' shanty.)

A digression here before we entertain the subject of camps, Great and otherwise. In the Adirondacks, the word "camp" carries considerable weight; elsewhere summer homes might be called cabins or cottages, but here such things are camps. Indeed, many tried to describe the ineffable nature of the Adirondack summer retreat. William Frederick Dix, editor of *Town and Country*, contributed an essay to *The Independent* in 1903 that touched on the simple allure of these camps to the world-weary men of affairs: "An Adirondack camp does not mean a canvas tent or a bark wigwam but

The Pine Knot compound, photographed by Seneca Ray Stoddard.
(Courtesy of the Adirondack Collection of the Saranac Lake Free Library)

a permanent summer home where the fortunate owners assemble for several weeks each year and live in perfect comfort and even luxury, tho' in the very heart of the woods, with no very near neighbors, no roads and no danger of intrusion. ... the truest type is composed of a group of rustic buildings on the edge of a lake, with pathless forests in the rear. Few who have not lived this healthful, invigorating life can appreciate its wonderful charm."

Harvey Kaiser, whose comprehensive book, *Great Camps of the Adirondacks* (1982) catalogues dozens of the remarkable structures, wrote a shorter piece for *Old House Journal* that summarized the Great Camp gestalt. The woodland retreats were not merely spaces enclosed by branches and bark, they engendered a lifestyle and particular response to the environment. Some — most notably the Durant camps — were self-sufficient villages (not unlike Fort Crown Point, perched on the thin edge of civilization), with well-conceived

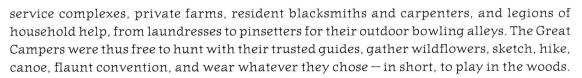

Durant's Kamp Kill Kare
(Courtesy of The Adirondack Museum)

service complexes, private farms, resident blacksmiths and carpenters, and legions of household help, from laundresses to pinsetters for their outdoor bowling alleys. The Great Campers were thus free to hunt with their trusted guides, gather wildflowers, sketch, hike, canoe, flaunt convention, and wear whatever they chose — in short, to play in the woods.

The camps that Durant conceived and sold to millionaires Collis P. Huntington, J. P. Morgan, and Alfred G. Vanderbilt all included a substantial parcel of land. Both Morgan's Camp Uncas and Vanderbilt's Sagamore were close to sixteen hundred acres, set on their own pristine, private lakes, far from prying eyes. In the grand sweep of Vanderbilt family property, though, Sagamore was small potatoes. Commodore Cornelius Vanderbilt, Alfred G.'s great-grandfather, left an estate of a hundred million dollars when he died in 1877, which was roughly equivalent to the sum total then in the coffers of the U.S. Treasury, and his scions were at the top of the fabulously wealthy class.

To others who would build Great Camps under the direction of New York–trained architects, the property surrounding Uncas and Sagamore were mere neighborhoods, not fiefdoms. At the turn of this century, the amount of land associated with the greatest of the Great Camps and the soignée forest park associations (which looked like Great Camps, with their collections of tastefully executed rustic buildings) was staggering. The Adirondack League Club was launched in 1890 with the purchase of more than 90,000 acres near Old Forge, and eventually reached 128,000 acres. (It now owns about 53,000 acres.) William Seward Webb, Alfred G. Vanderbilt's brother-in-law, acquired a whopping 115,000 acres for his camp, Nehasane, which included several large lakes and much of the Beaver River watershed. (Webb's fortune came from railroads, and in 1892 he built the Adirondack line of the New York Central. Nehasane's main lodge wasn't rustic at all and resembled an oversize suburban train depot.) William C. Whitney and lumberman Patrick Moynehan systematically spent three years in the mid-1890s buying up small tracts to consolidate some 70,000 acres for Whitney Park, north of Long Lake. The tract included Camp Cedars — a true rustic gem — built by William West Durant's cousin Frederick.

Camp Cedars. Photograph of the main building by Margaret Bourke-White, 1933.
(Courtesy of The Adirondack Museum)

Clearly there was more at stake here than creating a private getaway among the pines. Timbering provided a steady source of income for some of the estates: Webb — who hired Gifford Pinchot as a consultant in 1893 — was one of the first in the nation to attempt scientific, sustained-yield forestry. (He also tinkered with establishing a herd of elk, but this proved less successful than cutting spruce. The creatures didn't respect his blazed boundaries and succumbed to exposure or died from lead poisoning administered by large-caliber Winchesters.) Although these estates were remote, the nascent trend toward forging a backwoods industry was not hidden from the public. *Town and Country* editor Frederick Dix looked on the moneymaking camps as "highly significant as a phase of American life. This Adirondack wilderness is not merely a vast playground for the rich, not merely a haunt for the fisherman, not merely an exclusive pleasure preserve where money is lavished in great hotels, elaborate villas and luxurious camps, too far away to be accessible to the general public, but a mighty object lesson in forestry and a source of wealth to the state and the country."

18

At other Great Camps, especially in the St. Regis and Saranac lakes area, the emphasis was less on making the property pay than entertaining lavishly in fantastic settings. Many of these distinguished structures were designed by architect William Coulter, who moved to the region in the 1890s, not because of potential business, but because he suffered from tuberculosis. At that time, Saranac Lake was a center for treating the disease, and under the care of Dr. Edward Livingston Trudeau, William Coulter lived long enough to leave an outstanding legacy.

Echo Camp, photographed by Seneca Ray Stoddard in 1885. (Courtesy of The Adirondack Museum)

One of Coulter's early assignments in the rustic style was to design a game room at Sagamore, but he quickly made apparent his own considerable flair for native materials and innovative layouts. His most visible clients, on Upper Saranac Lake, included the leading Jewish businessmen of the time: for Otto Kahn, Coulter created the three-story Tudor-style lodge at Bull Point, but made the main house and guest buildings Adirondack rather than suburban by using logs and bark; for financier Adolph Lewisohn, he built Prospect Point, with a massive white birch bark-sided lodge as its centerpiece; for a group of families at Knollwood, he created six similar-sized lodges that each had different rustic embellishments; and for former Vice President Levi Morton, Coulter built two Great Camps, one on shore and one on Eagle Island, which used a series of complicated walkways and soaring interior spaces that blended with the site.

On the St. Regis lakes, not far from old Paul Smith's Hotel, Great Camps were built in abundance by architects from New York City and the Adirondacks, showing a variety of influences beyond native sticks and stones. Some were Japanese inspired, others had English cottage details such as eyebrow windows and roofs that looked like thatch, but the most elaborate of all was Marjorie Merriweather Post's Topridge. Some five dozen buildings — ranging from drab servants' apartments to sleeping cottages with Flamenco ruffles and frills, to a Russian dacha big enough for square dancing, to a palatial main lodge with a living room measuring about four thousand square feet — hugged the esker that gave the camp its name. Rooms were decorated in a dizzying eclectic array of animal skins (including chairs upholstered in leopard and zebra skin), antlers, Navajo rugs, horns, brass, silver, and whatever else Mrs. Post Close Hutton (as in E. F.) Davies (as in the ambassador to Russia prior to World War II) May selected in her many jaunts and junkets. Mrs. Post was the original party gal, and when she was at the lake, some eighty servants were there too.

The adventures of the Great Campers did not go unnoticed in the press. *Harper's Weekly* called the St. Regis estates "Camping de Luxe" in a generously illustrated 1906 feature. Newspapers also eagerly reported on life at Pine Knot and Sagamore: a headline in Utica's *Saturday Globe* in November 1908 proclaimed the Vanderbilt place to be a "Beautiful Adirondack Camp Where Luxury and Rustic Simplicity Are Combined." Major magazines like *House and Garden*, *Beautiful Homes*, and *Ladies Home Journal* trumpeted the Adirondack style and gave helpful hints on how to achieve it — albeit on a more modest scale. Indian artifacts were especially appropriate, they suggested, and proved to be readily available in the North Country. Since the 1890s, Iroquois families had camped in Saratoga each summer to sell baskets, mats, bows and arrows, and trinkets. Abenaki groups traveled to hotels and camps from Old Forge to Tupper Lake offering similar handmade wares. By 1906, in Lake Placid, there was a well-established shop on Main Street advertising Southwestern baskets, dolls, blankets, and rugs for camp decor.

People just could not get enough of this back-to-nature approach, and the concept of a distinct Adirondack style in architecture and furniture was nationally recognized by 1910, perhaps even better known than it is today. Books of plans for log cabins proliferated, beginning with *Log Cabins: How to Build and Furnish Them*, written by William S.

Interior of one of the Knollwood Club cottages.
(Courtesy of The Adirondack Museum)

Female tuberculosis patients slept in rustic tents near Saranac Lake.
(Photograph by Katherine McClellan, courtesy of Smith College Archives, Northampton, Mass)

Wicks in 1889 (and later reprinted by Dr. William Bruette and others). A half-dozen imitators followed, showing floor plans, elevations, and interiors, but Wicks's book outlasted them all. It underwent ten printings and is still available today, proving that some ideas are timeless indeed.

Tastes change, and inevitably, the Great Camp style — and the attendant costs of maintaining it — proved excessive. After the Depression, some estates were subdivided and sold, and many fell into disrepair or burned. Some — like Kahn's Bull Point — were torn down. A new generation looked at their grandparents' twig tables and used them for kindling to make room for Danish modern. Buildings once covered with spruce or birch bark became infested with insects and were sided with something generic that required less upkeep. In the 1960s it seemed that rustic architecture and furniture were in grave danger of becoming mere historical footnotes to a quaint and outmoded lifestyle. In the early 1970s, burdened by property taxes, insurance costs, extensive repairs, and other concerns, Camps Santanoni and Nehasane were sold to New York State. Webb's lodge was torn down, but the impressive lakeside buildings at Santanoni remain. In the late 1970s, Camp Sagamore — its acreage reduced to a tiny fraction of the former estate — was purchased by a nonprofit group that began a labor of love to bring the complex back to its former glory.

 *Sagamore Lodge*
(Courtesy of the Adirondack Collection of the Saranac Lake Free Library)

The sale of Sagamore was a clarion call to document the remaining Great Camps, and to begin nomination procedures to place some of them on the National Trust for Historic Places. One event in particular may have launched widespread interest in all things twig and bark: the 1976 exhibition of rustic furniture at the Adirondack Museum, which assembled hundreds of interesting pieces from all over the Northeast. Putting old shaggy things in the spotlight and on a pedestal gave new respect and new meaning to a time-honored expression of the Adirondack woods.

Today, the search for Adirondack style is enjoying a long-deserved renaissance. It embodies an homage to the past and a fusion with the future, where innovative designers take simple, natural materials to new heights and thoughtful owners use painstaking care to preserve unique properties. Read on.

CONTEMPORARY

INTERPRETATIONS

(previous page)   *This marshland lodge, located on the East Coast,
was designed by the cutting-edge firm of Centerbrook Architects in
Essex, Connecticut. The clients asked that it be rustic and one of a
kind, startling, full of fun, and able to sleep more than twenty guests.
There is a village-like quality to this house. Its design is based on the
principles of Adirondack architecture but it has moved a step beyond, into a fantasy rustic.*
(Photograph © Norman McGrath)

*The architectural firm of Bohlin Cywinski Jackson won an A.I.A.
National Honor award for its "urbane interpretation of the log vernacular" as seen in this timber complex in Maryland. The client
expressed a desire for something in the Adirondack spirit. Pavilions
loosely follow the course of a semicircular log wall set on a rocky out-
cropping. The structures are reminiscent of lean-tos, but are post
and beam construction. The log work is cut from white cedar, the siding
is red cedar, and the window walls have been framed in mahogany.*
(Photograph by Karl A. Backus)

24

IF YOU HAVE SPENT THE NIGHT IN A GUIDE'S TENT OR A LEAN–TO BUILT OF SLABS OF BARK, YOU HAVE LODGED IN A "CAMP." *If you chance to know a millionaire, you may be housed in a cobblestone castle, tread on Persian rugs, bathe in a marble tub, and retire by electric light — and still your host may call his mountain home a "camp." The applications of the word have been made so broad and various that exact definition has become impossible. It can only be said that "camp" in Adirondack parlance, has become a loose term applied indiscriminately to anything from a tent to a palace erected in the woods, in more or less isolation, primarily for pleasure and summer recreation. The word traces back, of course, to the log camps of the early lumberjacks — those rough buildings of unpeeled logs laid lengthwise and chinked at the point of contact with sticks and moss to keep out the cold.*

ALFRED DONALDSON • HISTORY OF THE ADIRONDACKS • 1921

Contemporary interpretations of the Adirondack camp are being hewn in log, stone, and wrought iron by the hands of a new generation of builders and craftsmen. They have in common with their predecessors the trait of fusing rustic with the luxurious and integrating modern convenience with the vernacular of this charming style. Some of the camps in this book reflect the original camp dynamic and pay tribute to the tradition. Others are the result of a designer digesting the elements of "Adirondack" and translating them into a structure that is a permutation of the style, further broadening the definition of camp.

The new camp designers follow in the path cleared by William West Durant. Alfred Donaldson wrote of Camp Pine Knot, the first Great Camp, "Before it there was nothing like it; since then despite infinite variations, there has been nothing essentially different from it." Vague perhaps, but an accurate statement nonetheless. There is an unbroken chain in the tradition of camp building. What began with Durant in the mid-1800s was advanced at the turn of the century by architect William Coulter, who brought his own vision and expertise to the creation of the Great Camps. He magnified the scale, and added to the repertoire a Tudor style intimated by half-logs and birch bark (instead of half-timber and stucco), decorative shingle work, and a sleeping porch.

Hole's Camp at the Ausable Club; photograph taken by George Wood, circa 1886.
(Courtesy of The Adirondack Museum)

25

Coulter took on two partners, Max Westhoff and William Distin, Sr., who continued the tradition, each broadening the firm's range. Westhoff refined the Swiss elements that Durant had introduced, and Distin perfected the rustic effect by experimenting with details: peeled logs, varied roof lines, and multiple-sided pavilions. Arthur Wareham came to work for Distin in the 1940s and was joined by Ron De Lair in the late 1960s. De Lair continues to practice at the firm known as Wareham-De Lair, where a young architect, Rich Hanpeter got his start. It is Hanpeter and his contemporaries who will extend the continuum and take this style into the next millennium.

The camps in this book are representative of what is currently taking place inside the Blue Line — the imaginary line that surrounds the Adirondack Park. However, the elements of Adirondack style extend all the way from Maine to California. This style has many visages: it can be seen in a Great Camp, a log cabin, a lean-to, a tuberculosis cure cottage, a Lake George Victorian, or a shingle-style home in the mountains. All of these have found their place in the Adirondacks historically and continue to be reproduced and improved upon by contemporary builders. Architectural scholars have attempted to list, categorize, and define camp, but because of its varied roots, it is a style that almost defies definition.

△ *This elegant home is referred to as a Second Empire Lake George Victorian. Originally built in 1890, it was moved from the adjoining property, and has recently undergone an extensive renovation and addition.*

◁ *View of the Lothrop Cabin at Camp Topridge. The owner and architect were aware that the scope of the renovation at Topridge required them to be sympathetic to the Adirondack spirit in form and materials. When completed, Topridge will be a village of spires, with some of the buildings exhibiting variations of northern European and Russian architecture. The flared roof and cupola of this building echo the Norwegian stave church. Vermont slate was cut to replicate the hips and valleys of the roof line. The copper sheathing has had a lead coating applied to subdue the glare and give the patina of age. Pine logs have been stained a pale gray to produce a blue-green tint. The architect was Richard Giegengack, and the contractor was Chris Tissot.*

A Primer on Camp Style

The concept of vacation home took hold in this country in the 1700s when colonists in the south came north to escape the steamy summer weather. The first vacation home in the Adirondacks was actually built in the 1760s along the Sacandaga River. In the early 1800s, settlers realized that beyond the Catskills there were mountains that boasted the highest peaks in the state. Following William Murray's seminal book *Adventures in the Wilderness*, came the rush of pleasure seekers and the need for shelter.

Originating as raised wood tent platforms intended to house outdoorsmen and their guides, "camps" eventually evolved into more permanent quarters. (Incidentally, these platforms are coming back as quirky additions to camp real estate and expanded sleeping quarters for guest overflow.) Due to the desire for solitude and a complete wilderness experience, building sites were remote and the roads reaching them were nearly impassable. Thus it was essential that the first camps be self-sufficient, since a jaunt to the market was inconceivable.

◁ *Inside a tent at Camp Wild Air.*
(Courtesy of The Adirondack Museum)

⋀ *Tent platforms at William Seward Webb's camp, Nehasane.*
(Courtesy of The Adirondack Museum)

An Adirondack Icon: The Lean-to

Probably the first Adirondack rustic structure to receive widespread recognition was the three-sided log lean-to. A lean-to is a primitive shelter protected from the elements, but with a large opening that allows the reclining occupant to take in a big view. As soon as tourist hunters and fishermen arrived on the scene in the early 1800s, guides began building temporary camps. The materials were readily at hand and the structures took only moments to put up. The earliest lean-tos were tepee-like sapling frameworks covered with sheets of bark; a bonfire faced the structure's open end to give light and heat as well as keep away predators. As guides returned to the same backcountry spots year after year, rectangular log lean-tos set on stone piers were erected.

By the 1930s, the Civilian Conservation Corps was building standardized lean-tos across the park, on hiking trails, and along waterways.

Nowadays, lean-tos are constructed as on-property sites for social gatherings.

➤ *The breezy living room at Lean-to Camp.*

➤ *Al fresco dining on the deck of Lean-to Camp.*

A Lean-to Camp in St. Huberts was built so the owners could spend time on their property and oversee the building of the barn and sleeping annex. What more could one need than a dry place to sleep, an outdoor deck for open-air dining, a small galley, a john, and, the dernier cri — an outdoor shower.

This lean-to has been properly chinked with moss and is brought up to date with electricity for lighting. Boughs were laid, stem down, and the furnishings placed on top, allowing the aromatic essence of the balsam mattress to surround the occupant. In the early years of camp the ladies slept on cushions stuffed with moss and the gentlemen slept on their carpetbags. Today, air mattresses and down pillows make roughing it more genteel.

The exteriors of the earliest camps had no architectural precedent — the structures were anomalies to the pure Victorian, Queen Anne, Romanesque, Beaux Arts, Arts and Crafts, and Art Nouveau styles of that era. These structures possessed four walls, roofs and an occasional reference to a Queen Anne turret or Arts and Crafts paneling. They had their own dialect and were urban man's interpretation of a woodland home. However, interiors and furnishings did reference these genres as is evident in photographs showing Victorian tufted sofas and Arts and Crafts lighting.

It is not clear whether or not architects were employed to design some of the first camps, although a recent discovery of drawings now in the possession of The Adirondack Museum indicates that Durant may have consulted with New York architect Grosvenor Atterbury on Camp Uncas. At any rate it is safe to assume that at the dawn of the Great Camp era many of the builders and local craftsmen carried with them knowledge from previous work, and that an architect's stamp did not appear on many plans if, in fact, plans existed. It wasn't until the involvement of cosmopolitan architectural firms like McKim, Mead and White; Davis McGrath and Shepard; and John Russell Pope that pure rustic became infused with current trends in architecture.

Durant's Camp Pine Knot was comprised of a compound of small individual buildings, each with its own function. By the time Pine Knot was completed there were twenty-seven buildings. These structures were connected by covered walkways to protect the visitor from inclement weather. This plan provided privacy and, in the event of fire, it isolated trouble. The buildings at Pine Knot were a combination of spruce log and frame construction with cedar bark sheathing. Some of the buildings had bay windows and some had stoops; others had actual porches. The interior walls were varied — stained pine planking, vertical bead board, or the flat hewn backside of logs filled with plaster in between. Durant experimented with birch bark as a wall covering and continued to use it throughout his career.

In subsequent projects, Durant was on a quest for a larger, more sophisticated showcase in which to entertain his city friends. He played with new forms and materials, always pushing the style a little further. At Uncas, he graduated to stone foundations and log construction, in which the log ends were mitered, not notched as in his first project. For the first time he employed an open floor plan. At Sagamore, Durant added refinements not yet seen in many city homes, including gas, water, and a central heating system so that the camp could be used year-round. The main lodge — a grand, three-story chalet — was a logistical feat in frame construction overlaid with spruce slab. Other early camps like Santanoni, Cedars, and Fairview were of uniform horizontal log construction reminiscent of fortresses, especially the latter two, which possess one-story entries flanked by two-story towers.

➤ *The nursery at Pine Knot. On the steps: Janet Durant with nurse and baby Basil. Photograph by Seneca Ray Stoddard, 1890.* (Courtesy of The Adirondack Museum)

By 1910, most camps were being designed with a single larger "lodge" and multiple support buildings. The main lodge was a multipurpose structure and featured a great room for socializing, kitchen and dining areas, and multiple rooms to accommodate guests. Ceilings were raised and vaulted with elaborate and stout truss systems. Because the medicinal benefits of the mountain air had become apparent, porches were added as outdoor living spaces. Roofs were extended to provide protection from weather: as a result interiors were dark to the extreme. The outbuildings ranged in size and purpose and could include anything from a boathouse to a pumphouse.

 *The main approach from the boathouse looking up to the dining hall at Prospect Point, circa 1904.*

This camp exemplifies William Coulter's synthesis of rustic with Tudor in his work and includes elements of Bavarian and Japanese architecture.
(Courtesy of The Adirondack Museum)

William Coulter was the man who drove this transformation of the rustic style. The apex was Coulter's rendition of a grand lodge for financier Adolph Lewisohn. The architect had upped the ante in scale and complexity that began with his work for the Trudeau sanatorium, was perfected at the Knollwood Club, and culminated at Lewisohn's Prospect Point on Upper Saranac Lake. This camp, built in 1903, was as grandiose and flamboyant as its owner, and resembled not one but four massive Bavarian chalets capped by broad gabled roofs with flared ends and connected by enclosed walkways. Unpeeled spruce log siding was used on the lower story; the overlapping upper story had slab siding cut in a picket fence pattern. Coulter employed his tried and true mock-Tudor style, using half-logs and birch bark under the gable eaves. He interjected Japanese flavor in the form of crossed boards known as *chigi* that extended beyond the roofline. The interior walls were horizontal plank wainscoting of southern pine. This masterpiece was a tour de force and cost over $2.5 million by the time Lewisohn was sated.

Interestingly, in 1916 the Adirondack lodge style of architecture was adopted by the National Park Service for their structures, thus making this regional manner of building familiar to people across the country (although not necessarily by name).

After World War I, there was a dramatic reduction in the number of buildings at a typical camp. For William Rockefeller's Camp Wonundra, architect William Distin created a large living and dining pavilion with three radiating wings for bedrooms and services. (This camp is now the luxury hotel, The Point. Because it has been a refuge for the wealthy since 1986 and one of the few Great Camps that remains opulently appointed, it has been the springboard for many of the new camps being designed today.)

The Great Camp building era waned with the Depression. However, two camps were built post-Depression, Eagle Nest and Minnowbrook — both designed by William Distin.

Following World War II, Americans were preoccupied with establishing their careers, families, and primary residences. "Pulling their socks up" after the war, they had no time to think about their vacation homes. There was a serious shortage of building materials in the country and the major highways leading into the park were still relatively primitive. In the 1960s, a peppering of new camps were built in the Adirondack Park. It was, however, the age of the dreadful A-frame chalet and knotty pine prefab, which bore little resemblance to Durant's magnificent camps.

The decade from 1970 to 1980 defied precedent. The creative intelligentsia and design eminents who were dictating trends in this country forged ahead into uncharted terri-

A recently renovated bedroom at The Point, a Relais & Chateaux property on Upper Saranac Lake.

tory and never looked back. As unappealing as many of the fashions and home designs might be to our eyes today, they were, at the very least, innovative. The concept of a vacation home to the generation building at the time was a contemporary, angular structure with large windows, likely to have clapboard siding and a deck. Many resembled the prow of a ship. Since energy was a major concern, cyclopean windows and skylights were installed for passive-solar heating. A multitude of these ark-like structures dot the landscape. Not native to any area in particular, this design has fallen out of favor with the current generation of second home buyers who are looking for a living experience authentic to a region and its past.

In the early 1980s, the "Country" movement began. This trend became a lifestyle that borrowed heavily from the past and paved the way for the return to the Adirondack tradition of camp building. In the mid-1980s, a chosen few from a generation who had summered in older camps built their vacation homes in the image of the Great Camps. This was a highly educated group — visually and stylistically more savvy than their parents — weaned on a flow of images that paraded the prescribed fashion, home decor, and lifestyle dictums du jour. Most importantly, they were a financially secure bunch, inclined to hire visionary architects to create the woodland homes that spoke of the history of the Adirondacks. This phenomenon occurred primarily on the eastern side of the park and drew its steam from New York, Philadelphia, and Boston. Ground zero for the return to a regional rustic architecture can be traced to 1986 when two families, one in Hague on Lake George and one at the Ausable Club in St. Huberts, designed their homes, unbeknownst to each other, in the Great Camp tradition. These camps were followed by others, and by the late 1990s, the architects and builders specializing in rustic were as busy as their forebears had been one hundred years before.

◁ Built in 1986 on the site of a cabin owned by a painter, the stone pergola and boathouse were the only remaining structures integrated into the new plan for this camp. It is a brilliant fusion of Adirondack Great Camp, Victorian, and Japanese architectural styles. The key design motif, a gable detail known as a barrel vault, is six feet deep and mirrors the elliptical window of the main lodge. This Victorian gable form is echoed in the boathouse and teahouse. The barrel vaults are lit from above so that at night, when traversing the lake, one sees three illuminated elliptical shapes.

Inside, the light play of the ellipsoid window on the great room (see page 2) starts at one side of the space and tracks around the room during the day "casting a curved organic light" on the oval-shaped upper gallery — a complex concept in architecture beautifully executed. This camp was designed by the architectural firm of Wareham-De Lair; the project architect was Rich Hanpeter; the builder was the late Karl Andreasson; and all branch work is by twig master Crispin Shakeshaft.

A profile of the new breed of Great Campers would suggest that they are captains of industry, famous actors and musicians, young turks of Wall Street, and doctors and lawyers. Some are from old money, others made it less than an hour ago. Nonetheless, the competition for bigger, better, and barkier is on — and it is a spectacle to behold.

As was the case during the building boom that occurred at the end of the 1800s, today the flourishing peacetime economy makes it possible for the wealthy to build their vacation homes indulgently. Whether it be on Georgica Pond in the Hamptons or on Raquette Lake in the Adirondacks, the economic and social similarities of this fin de siècle climate are startling.

The late-twentieth-century version of camp, however, is generally not on the grand scale of its predecessors, in part because of the limited availability of large parcels of land. Unlike the 1880s, when an unrestrained Durant or Vanderbilt was able to purchase two thousand acres in a single transaction, the State of New York and the larger timber companies are the primary purchasers of any vast acreage that becomes available today. In addition, there are many regulations and zoning laws pertaining to building inside the Blue Line that are enforced by the Adirondack Park Agency or local authorities. Finally, the expense of maintaining a camp the magnitude of Sagamore is beyond prohibitive—heat, hired help, and maintenance are on a different wage scale than they were a century ago, and to employ a staff of up to forty is inconceivable. Camps of this proportion are not likely to be recreated in today's world. To put this in perspective, even the largest camps built today are only a quarter the size of Sagamore.

◄ *The Dacha at Topridge, built in the 1930s, is a reminder that one of the four husbands of Marjorie Merriweather Post (its most illustrious owner) was an ambassador to Russia.*

The Adirondack style continues to be dictated by indigenous materials, notably log and stone, and by the severe weather of the region. It is not uncommon to have a temperature of -40 degrees Fahrenheit, and sixteen feet of snow is typical for an Old Forge winter. These factors result in the building of structures that are in perfect harmony with their surroundings and totally appropriate for a woodland setting and northern climate. In these camps one can see evidence of rustic mountain architecture of Swiss, Bavarian, Scandinavian, Russian, and Japanese inspiration — these regions share similar topography and extreme weather conditions.

As in all creative endeavors, architectural style is influenced by what has come before it, the designer's visual vocabulary, and a response to the setting. The new Adirondack style attempts to evoke the past and refers to it often in structure and furnishings — the mantra is "authenticity." At the same time it incorporates the advances made in architecture during the past century (Frank Lloyd Wright and Ludwig Mies van der Rohe, for example), Adirondack style unites contemporary concepts and its Victorian-era antecedents. Although at times it can be cliché-ridden and kitschy, it is often brilliant.

Three Timbers, as seen from the lake. The name Three Timbers was chosen by the owners in deference to the Holy Trinity, and throughout the camp, a decorative reference to three is used. The architectural firm of Wareham-De Lair with Rich Hanpeter as project architect designed this home. Bob Becker was the builder. Hanpeter designed the camp so that all rooms look out onto the lake. The design of this camp is probably the most Adirondack in inspiration of any of his camp projects. It revisits the platform camps of the 1800s, with separate spaces for living room, kitchen, and bedroom, all connected by walkways.

EXTERIOR DETAILS: FROM THE FOUNDATION UP

Until recently, the construction season in the Adirondacks was limited to the late summer and early fall months, when it was relatively dry and snowless. Now contractors are capable of building year-round. Recently a camp on Upper St. Regis Lake was built under the protection of a heated tennis bubble so that three work crews could labor around the clock in a protected environment. This was ideal for several reasons: the climatically controlled space provided comfort to the workers during a brutally cold winter, protected and seasoned the materials, and allowed for the completion of the camp before another summer went by. But year-round building projects need not be this extreme; in most cases, equipment and techniques are such that all but foundations can be worked on at any time of year.

Many camps that are not winterized have no foundation. These structures are raised on log pilings or stone piers that have been sunk deep into the ground. Decorative skirting has been added to discourage animals from nesting, and to enable air to circulate underneath the building, keeping dampness to a minimum. The pilings on older camps inevitably get replaced, but today an increased life span can be expected with the use of pressure-treated lumber.

◅ *The road entrance to Camp Topridge is as beguiling as the lakeside one. This camp was first built in 1897. Marjorie Merriweather Post purchased it in 1920 and set about creating a village of sixty-eight structures. She was inclined toward the colorful, and fancied Indian, Russian, and Norwegian themes. Mrs. Post lived lavishly in the woods and employed a staff of eighty-five when at camp. The stories of her escapades have reached legendary status in the Adirondacks.*

Topridge was in and out of private ownership until 1994, when it was sold to a family that has taken on the herculean project of rescuing the property from its distressed condition. The renovation for the main lodge was based on the boathouse and its organic branch work (see page 75); the flared elephant-foot cedar trademark was used throughout.

➤ *When standing on the gazebo of this porch at Camp Windrush, which looks out over Spitfire Lake, it feels as if one is on a yacht. The branch skirting is ancient and interesting.*

Stonework

Stones pulled from the water or ground near a job site — notably river rock, fieldstone, and cut or hewn granite — have always been employed as foundation and fireplace material. In the eastern Adirondacks, limestone and granite are available; in the northeastern Adirondacks, a hard red sandstone; and in the central Adirondacks, builders use glacially shaped boulders of anorthosite, a granular rock composed of soda-lime feldspar. As building designs become more intricate and owners strive for individuality, more unusual materials are being imported, and stone is no exception. Exotic granites, marbles, and stones are being brought in from all over the world. In a climate where snow sits on the ground six months of the year and segues into two months of mud season before finally becoming summer, stone is ideal for protecting a structure from dampness and rot. It can be hand laid or put into concrete. Architect Rich Hanpeter uses stone splash beds around the perimeter of structures to make the building look firmly seated in the ground.

➢ *An exterior view of Bearhurst on Lake Pleasant in Speculator. When visiting Lake Pleasant as a child, current owner Helen Armstrong rowed across the lake to see this magnificent home, and returned to tell her parents of her discovery. Her mother, who had set aside $500 for the purchase of a fur coat, used it instead as a down payment on the camp.*

Bearhurst was built for Herman Meyrowitz in 1894 and has been exceptionally well maintained by the Armstrongs. The camp is constructed of full log with a combination of vertical and horizontal placement. There are a number of cabins on this property that are rented out to vacationers.

◅ *This camp on Echo Pond in Lake Placid was originally built as a woodland getaway in the late 1920s. It was a destination for revelers who skied out on the Whitney Trail to cook pancakes on the griddle. This site has also been a featured location in several old movies. The original stones for this camp were pulled from the Ausable River by the owner and her contractor. This would not be looked upon favorably by the Department of Environmental Conservation today, but there were enough old stone walls and fieldstone nearby that a seamless transition of stone was made possible when the new wing was added.*

Stonework is, by nature, labor-intensive work; it is therefore also expensive. A fireplace rising one story can cost an average of $15,000. If granite, slate, or fieldstone are used on the exterior, it is always pleasing to incorporate it somewhere in the interior of the camp, such as an entry area or hearth — making for a cohesive and unified whole.

Brick is rarely seen in the Adirondacks, because the soil is too sandy to make brick. Very few historic homes used it in facades, and firebrick for fireplaces was imported from outside the region.

A weathered rock retaining wall was added to this property to reinforce the element of stone found in the original pergola (left) that remains on the site. These are dry-laid stones, by far the most visually impressive and time-consuming mode of masonry. Tucked beneath the driveway are a root cellar and planting room that break up the horizontal line of the stone wall.

The pergola is a paradise in the summer, when the clematis and grapevines are in bloom.

Siding

Historically, Adirondack builders have paraded their expertise by experimenting with different woods and types of siding. At Longwood on Upper St. Regis Lake, built in 1906, the beams, studs, and sills were of hemlock; the rafters were of peeled spruce; the siding on the upper story was of cedar bark sheathing; and the roof was cedar shingle. They took risks by using unorthodox materials considered unacceptable or lowly, and made them fashionable. Today, builders and designers looking for a fresh approach adhere to no rules and are constantly trying to achieve the visual double-take.

A general rule of thumb in camp building is that anything structural has the potential to be ornamental (this includes the cross-bracing of log extensions, trusswork, etc.). One is limited only by the imagination. Something as simple as a notched log has multiple variations, intended not so much to achieve a better notch, but for a more decorative result. When a woodworker is fashioning unmilled wood, nature and caprice dictate the outcome.

A description of the most popular siding materials being used inside and outside in traditional and contemporary buildings follows.

Log: Logs provide excellent insulation and retain heat. By the end of the Great Camp era, however, the supply of large logs for oversized structures was depleted, and it was necessary to bring logs of this girth and length from Canada. For Camp Wonundra, pine logs 18-to-20 inches in diameter were needed and had to be imported. Today most logs used in construction are imported to the site, and the western United States (notably Montana and Wyoming) has become a source for red cedar and lodgepole pine, which is massive and, more important, straight.

Half-log: A self-descriptive siding, this is a half-round log with bark intact that is applied to a framed structure. Sometimes the ends are left whole and notched to masquerade as a full-log structure. Often camps that appear to be

⋀ Built in 1873, this is one of the oldest homes in the High Peaks region. The design of the structure, built of unpeeled cedar log, recalls a rustic rural Scandinavian architecture. It is believed that the inspiration for the camp came from a book or travel correspondence. The owner, a man named Matthews, was the inventor of the soda fountain and most of the cast bronze handles on doors and furniture were faucet handles originally made for his carbonating machines.

◅ The bullet-notch detail is unusual (if not dangerous) and illustrates an example of a Swedish cope. Note the scalloped metal edging used to secure the bark around the door frame.

log structures are, in fact, frame-built with half-round logs or applied bark sheathing.

Unpeeled log: If bark is meant to stay on the log, the trees should be cut between November and the end of January. Unpeeled logs are generally used while green and, in the case of homes in the Adirondack Park, white cedar is most commonly used. It is indigenous to the North Country and can be found in diameters up to 10 inches. Because of the labor involved in locating this wood, it is more expensive. Cedar is favored because its heartwood is resistant to rot and bug infestation. Spruce, Ponderosa pine, white pine, and red pine are also appropriate.

Peeled log: Spruce or cedar are top choices. The tree should be felled in the summer, when the bark is loose and easily removed. Western red cedar comes from the log kit and lumber companies of the West and is available in diameters up to 18 inches. Should a natural finish be desired on peeled log exterior siding, a clear penetrating sealant should be used; otherwise a semitransparent stain with a wood-tone tint will deepen the hue, act as a preservative, and provide protection from mildew and bugs. Interior peeled logs can be finished in hand-rubbed Danish or linseed oil. Historically, at Sagamore and other Great Camps, beeswax was applied and rubbed to a high polish.

Camp Gull Rock on Lake Placid is an excellent example of the use of unpeeled log. Designed by William Coulter, it has been lovingly restored by the new owner who has fully renovated the eleven buildings on the site. Note the "beaver-chewed" raised walkways that snake through the property, and customized pull cart — a whimsical creation of the caretaker.

Topridge's "Honeymoon Cabin," seen from across a bay, is a powerful blend of Alpine, Scandinavian, and Adirondack. The foundation and lower floor are granite; the upper floors are peeled red pine log, stained a light brown. The architect was Michael Bird and the contractor was Jack Levitt.

The exterior of Cedar Rock Ledge on Tupper Lake is sided with cedar shingles, and finished with rugged cedar railings. This camp was designed by Michael Bird and built by Schoolhouse Renovations.

Milled log siding: These are 2-by-8-inch boards that have been rounded to look like logs, with a separate rounded bead placed between the boards. This is a variation on the half-log theme, but more uniform in size and shape.

Board and batten/board and channel: Often rough-sawn, the former has a strip that has been applied to the place where boards are joined, the latter has a recess between the boards and a strip laid underneath at the joint. Board and batten was used as siding for typical Adirondack homes in the mid-1800s as an alternative to clapboard, which was not readily available. Until recently, this siding was very common in small camps and ordinary homes. A new take on this style is board and rough channel, where the top board is finished and rough bark remains on the recessed channel strip.

Stovewood walls: Traditionally found in other cold climate areas, these short lengths of cut logs (round or quartered) laid horizontally in mortar, round side facing out, are gaining new popularity in the Adirondacks.

Cedar shingle: Cedar is known for its resistance to insects as well as to weather, making any form of it suitable for this region. Cedar is particularly appropriate when rough-sawn. Cedar shake is the hand-split version of the shingle. It is rougher, less uniform, and therefore an ideal choice for a natural cladding.

Novelty siding: A lipped board that is often used on camp utility buildings because it doesn't require sheathing. The boards are lapped over one another, leaving a coved notch visible between the boards.

"V" Joint: Cedar or pine boards that, when fit together, leave a "V" groove between the boards. They should be applied vertically to allow for water drainage.

➤ *The annex at Lean-to Camp owes its heritage both to the early Adirondack frame-built farm style and to the Great Camp. Inside, each room has a fireplace, sleeping porch, and bathroom. Elizabeth Stewart, architectural and interior designer, and architect Reed Morrison found that the cruciform was the only formation that would allow for these accommodations. They used a nine-foot standard for ceiling height and eight-foot doors to play up the verticality of this space. Stewart has elevated the status of board and batten to a new level of respect with this camp. The builder was Baird Edmonds of Keene Valley.*

Clapboard and its humble cousin brainstorm: Finished clapboard of a 4-to-6-inch reveal was typical in local farmhouses. Brainstorm (alias "hog pen" and also known as Adirondack siding) are boards that have the live edge or bark left on one side. This lends an organic element to structures and can be applied to either exterior or interior walls for a great visual effect. As with most of the lore of the Adirondacks, there are two versions to every story and the origin of brainstorm is no exception. One rendition goes like this: brainstorming was originally the discard of the sawmills. Its use was thought up by a clever but indigent logger who had the notion — brainstorm — to use it on his own home. The other, more theatrical version involves marital infidelity and murder. At the turn of the century, Stanford White, the noted architect, was murdered by a man who claimed he became temporarily insane due to a "brain storm." His alleged insanity was said to have been caused by the excitement of encountering White, who had been romantically involved with the man's wife. In honor of this much-publicized defense ploy, Ben Muncil, a talented camp builder, and millwright Charles Nichols developed this new siding as an alternative to clapboard and felt that its inception was the result of a similar mental event.

Slab siding: This first pass off the tree at the mill is difficult to work with, and generally still has the bark on. It varies in width from 4-to-6 inches wide by 0-to-4 inches thick (thin at the edge and thicker in the center as it curves into a half round shape). Boards must be placed carefully, so that they fit tightly on the sheathing while still allowing for variety in geometric detailing.

A room at The Point demonstrates the interior use of brainstorm siding.

➤ *This boathouse on Lake Placid features the combination of sawtooth-end vertical slab and brainstorm siding that is a signature of builder Peter Torrance.*

Twig Work and Bark

Rustic decoration became popular in England in the form of garden accessories, gazebos, arbors, and furniture. In the late 1700s, there were many pattern books published in the vein of *Ideas for Rustic Furniture* (1780) that gave patterns for twig pieces that were heavily influenced by Chinese bamboo furnishings. These were interpreted for the American market in the mid-1800s. When Frederick Law Olmsted designed Central Park in the heart of New York City, he called for up to twenty rustic twig structures. The embellishment of camps with twig work began with Pine Knot. With its medley of natural elements — unpeeled limbs and branches used for ornamental railings, birch and cedar bark sheathing on framed construction, decorative twig ornamentation enthusiastically applied throughout — Pine Knot was an essay in rustica.

The weaving and working of branch and sapling is boundless in its potential. Twig work is tedious, and requires patient and knowledgeable craftsmen to build lasting, bug-free construction assembled with tight joints and an artful hand; it is not for the amateur.

The lyrical name of this camp has been enunciated in twig on the gable screen by builder Guy Schweizer.

Noted Great Camp architect William Coulter employed the decorative open-log-work gable screen in his buildings and it became his signature, as seen at the Knollwood Club circa 1903. This decorative approach served two functions: it kept a breeze circulating, thus cooling the interior, and it brought more light to the inside spaces.
(Courtesy of The Adirondack Museum)

Putting bark to work as sheathing traces its ancestry, in this country, to the Indian wigwam. As a decorative detail for Great Camps and their descendants, bark provides an opportunity to introduce diversity in color and texture to an exterior. The bark of cedar (medium brown, tight, and shaggy), spruce (darker brown, tight, not so shaggy), hemlock (mixed brown, crusty looking) or birch (white or yellow with dark dash-like markings) is stripped from the tree in sheets. It is left to dry flat for days and then tacked to siding or used as an embellishment. It requires no special treatment and is essentially maintenance free, but longevity is increased if protected by an overhang. Replacement parts are only a tree away.

➤ A suspension footbridge conceived and built by Jamie Sutliffe for the Long Lake Camp for the Arts.

Interestingly, most of the exterior siding materials mentioned have been used on interior walls too, which can be very textural and visually appealing. Many of these materials would be considered unconventional to builders elsewhere, but the Adirondacks is a place with a history of architectural and decorative experimentation.

⋎ Red and Nan La Fountaine at their Lake Placid cottage. A large sun was painted on the porch deck after a particularly long and grim winter that, according to the artist, seemed like nine months without sun. All of the porch soffit ornamentation was created by the owner.

⋎ This twig arbor was given to the owners by builder Peter Torrance as a present for their daughter's wedding, which was held at this camp on Lake Placid.

Roofs, Windows, and Doors

A flattened roof pitch of 4-over-12 (which refers to the rise and run — the pitch of the roof expressed as a vertical increase in height for a selected distance in the horizontal direction) was borrowed from the Swiss. This pitch allowed the roof to hold the snow as insulation during the winter months. Broad overhangs of the roof kept melting snow and rain away from the foundation and protected the siding.

The entrance to the Bissell Camp is in keeping with the Durant tradition of covered walkways. Owner Chip Bissell, in partnership with builder Peter Torrance, created a protected entrance of peeled cedar. This type of decorative railing has become Torrance's trademark, a style he began working on twenty years ago when renovating an older camp. The camp is capped with multiple roof lines, which play sharp angles against the unpredictable forms of nature. The siding is a pleasing mixture of vertical slab with picket fence edge on the upper story layered over horizontal sheathing. This zigzag pattern is echoed in the lower siding, railings, door, and side lights.

Multiple roof lines are characteristic of modern camps, and they can vary in pitch, overhang, and style. A traditional peak on one level leading to a hipped roof on another can move a camp design from insipid to captivating. Nowadays, roof pitches of 8-over-12 to 12-over-12 are the norm, and are important in helping snow and rain to run off the roof. Saranac Lake architect Michael Bird feels that odd roof pitches look better (for

Lean-to Camp barn designed by Elizabeth Stewart. A simple yet striking structure, made so by the whimsy of the 12-over-12 with a 6-over-12 "broken pitch" roof and the concise use of color.

example, 5-over-12, 7-over-12, 9-over-12). Bird designs his roof pitches so that they become steeper as they go up. Likewise, his overhangs decrease in depth as they ascend — deeper on the bottom, narrower on top. Taken together, the pitch and the overhang create the illusion of the height and branch arrangement of a towering pine. Overhangs should be built to provide shade in the summer, but not be so deep as to eclipse the low winter sun.

A common material used for roofing is cedar shingle. Builder Peter Torrance uses green asphalt shingles as cladding so that the roofline disappears into the foliage. Although slate roofs can be found in mid-19th century Champlain Valley homes and churches, they are rare in the heart of the Adirondacks. Steep roof pitches and sheet metal were often combined on early Adirondack structures. Sheet metal roofing, now available in myriad colors, can animate a facade and visually reinforce accent colors on door and trim.

Windows have been called the eyes of the house. From the outside they can bring vitality to a facade, and from the inside grant an inspirational view. Ideally they do both. In the early camps and cabins, windows were small: glass was hard to come by and difficult to replace, and since it was not an insulator, these small windows were a necessity for the long cold winters. In camps built in the twentieth century, stock windows and doors were purchased from millwork catalogs offering a vast assortment of styles. Some unconventional shapes crept into the vernacular. Diamond-shaped and diamond-pane windows were often used on the St. Regis camps and have become de rigueur in contemporary camp design. The use of small diamond-shaped windows at the upper gable level provided an architectural solution to the lack of light caused by wide overhangs and porches, and a counterpoint to the diamond pane. These windows have been adopted by today's designers, and have become a signature element for at least one. Eyebrow, triangular, and elliptical window shapes are also part of the camp vocabulary.

Unusually shaped windows can be the cornerstone around which a camp is designed. Today's camp designers and builders have the luxury of thermal-pane glass in as many sizes and shapes as one can imagine. In an effort to bring nature indoors, camps are being designed with many windows, little wall space (save for the upper level if opened to the second story), and expensive and heavy window treatments. As private as these retreats are, there can be a feeling of being exposed to the elements, due to the huge, dark expanses of glass opening out to the wilderness.

Shutters are not often seen on log-sided structures but are plentiful on the standard small cabin. These upright planks display cutout images of pine trees, half moons, deer, squirrels, and geometric Indian motifs. If northbound travelers aren't certain they have arrived in the Adirondacks, the shutters surely give it away.

➤ *This camp on a lake near Monticello, New York, was designed by Michael Bird and built by Steve Dubrovsky. The owners craved a camp in the Adirondacks, but the travel time would have been overwhelming. Instead they found a peaceful lakeside setting closer to home.*

A well-thought-out fenestration plan includes the addition of diamond windows tucked beneath the roof gables. This allows maximum light during the day and makes for a welcoming exterior at night.

The windows at Bearhurst are unrivaled in their beauty. They bring a kaleidoscopic interest and quality of light to the interior. This blue bottle window, made from bottle ends, gives an ocular impression. The piece was commissioned by Herman Meyrowitz, a tycoon who made his fortune in optics.

This window at Bearhurst depicts the insignia for the camp: a bear set into a cartouche along with the date the camp was built — 1894.

A remarkable window at Bearhurst that was set into the chimney to bring light directly into the master bedroom.

The front door of any dwelling provides the opportunity to make a grand statement. This can be conveyed through scale, choice of material, fenestration (treatment of the windows), hardware, or all of the above. The front door should capture the character of the camp and set the tone for the inside of the house. In his book *Camps in the Woods*, Gus Shepard called for doors to have five panels of pine with copper screens and heavy wrought iron fixtures, instead of the leather strapping that was used in the early log homes in the area. Wide, heavy boards were recommended to give the door some heft, allowing it to hold up to the weight of the structure.

Interior doors can vary, but a five-horizontal-paneled door is appropriate and can still be purchased from manufacturers' catalogs. Architectural salvage is also an option, as vintage doors from the turn of the century usually have more character than many of the current limited, uninspired offerings. Of course, custom doors are ideal and add a distinctive flair. Of the doors documented in this book, the custom doors were the most impressive due to their weight, thickness, and beefy hardware. They are aesthetically pleasing and make effective sound barriers.

> *This entry door was designed and created by Barney Bellinger of Sampson Bog Studio. It depicts an elaborate forest scene recreated in burned wood, twig, and birch.*

∧ *The screen door bear silhouette at Bearhurst was created by owner Dick Armstrong. An art glass window features beveled diamond panes. Although it appears to be part of the original camp, it was actually made within the last decade by Adirondack Stained Glass in Gloversville.*

➤ Forest-side entrance to the "Honeymoon Cabin" at Camp Topridge. Jamie Sutliffe carved a wildlife scene into the door depicting a resident loon among the cattails.

↖ A painted metal screen door is one of the few Indian-inspired details left from the Post days at Topridge.

◄ This window, vibrant in design and coloration, is part of the Dacha at Topridge.

◄ *This camp was the inspiration for this book. Designed by Bohlin Cywinski Jackson, the architects describe the property as follows: "The house becomes analogous to the forest, its stone base rising out of the hillside and tree columns extending upward toward a lead-coated copper roof which softly reflects the sky." Its structure is modeled on the residential camp complexes from the turn of the century, but the treatment is decidedly modern.* (Photograph by Karl A. Backus)

Color

Exterior color was traditionally limited to brown siding, whether it was natural bark or an oil stain, enhanced by colorful window frames and perhaps doors. The rationale was that brown would be unobtrusive and blend well with nature, but there was also limited availability of paints and stains. Johnsburg red and Johnsburg brown were both deep, dark paint colors made from minerals found in mountains near North Creek, and were widely used in the late 1890s.

The turn of the century brought more frequent, and creative, uses of color to exteriors. In an issue of *The Craftsman* magazine (published by Gustav Stickley) dated 1903, Harvey Ellis elaborated that "the exterior could be stained a dull orange tone, dull red on the shingled roof, purplish brown and gray on the slabs and would give coloration of a faded autumn leaf." This marked a high point in the imaginative use of color as a means of relating to the landscape.

Regarding the topic of trim and accent colors, early on Durant took the opportunity to introduce color in his window frames. As can be seen at Pine Knot and Sagamore, he most often used deep red. Green is popular today, specifically a dark shutter green, although the spectrum runs from hunter to lighter, mossier greens as well. Orange and yellow trims, while uncommon, are reminiscent of state campground signage; it is certain however, that these sunny colors will have their day again as the camp aesthetic evolves and revolves.

Contemporary designers have rethought the muddy spectrum used a century ago. They are including in their repertoire a lighter color scheme, featuring pale natural wood stains and khaki and gray semitransparent stain on siding, offset by accent colors in solid stain or oil paint. One Saranac Lake architect, Ron De Lair, traditionally uses four colors on the exteriors of camps: a beige tone semitransparent stain for siding, a mossy green accent color on the window frame in solid stain with window detail in darker green, and doors in copper verde or rural red (cranberry) enamel. He plays the colors against the degree of gloss — the high sheen is saved for the architectural focal point, the door. Another architect, Michael Bird, prefers materials to remain natural or close to it, allowing the structure to blend with its natural surroundings.

At Three Timbers, the unusual combination of green and blue trim on khaki was selected by architect Rich Hanpeter to suggest a watercolor of a tree (a palette that implies green leaves, blue sky, and tan bark). The three stacked brackets — or what is known as an outrigger form — illustrate the influence of Craftsman ideology on new projects.

The Bissell Camp under a sapphire northern sky on a bitter night in the Adirondacks.

Exterior Lighting

At Pine Knot, glass-enclosed kerosene lanterns wove a course through the property, illuminating walkways from building to building; many contemporary camps recreate that effect. Today, pathways winding through wooded areas are best lit by lantern-type lights on low posts that illuminate pesky roots and rocks and create an obvious trail. They give depth to a property in the darkness and act as a beacon from the lake. Front door and alternative entrances can also be lit with fixtures that befit a woodland setting — wrought iron or oxidized metals (such as copper and bronze) with tinted glass shades to eliminate glare. Rustic lighting design has expanded greatly in the last five years. Exterior lights that are ideal for camp include colonial lanterns, Craftsman, Prairie, and Mission styles. These are available in all price ranges and even through mail order.

The anticipation of entering the main lodge at Topridge is heightened by the imposing light fixtures that draw you to the front door. The wrought iron and art glass chandeliers were made by Bill Epps.

All of the exterior walkway lighting at Topridge was cast in bronze by Timeworks Unlimited. James Guy of Texas designed eight decorative panels to be used on the post lights throughout the camp. A balcony made for a young boy features fairy-tale carvings by Paul Stark.

This five-bedroom, three-bath boathouse on Lake George was built by George Reis and housed "El Lagarto," the champion speedboat of the late 1920s.

Boats and Boathouses

The waterways of the Adirondacks have long been resplendent with boats — from birch bark canoes and guideboats to steam launches and elegant motorboats. There is a hierarchy in boatdom on the lakes of the Adirondacks that began with the transition from steam to gas inboard engines. The steam launches popular in the 1870s and 1880s were followed by vessels that were powered by vaporized naphtha and electricity in the late 1890s. By 1910, gasoline-powered engines ruled the lakes; they were faster, more glamorous, and far more expensive than their predecessors. Boatbuilders like Hacker Craft, the Christopher Columbus Smith Boat and Engine Company (later known as Chris-Craft), Fay and Bowen Engine Company, Gar Wood, and a number of independents, cranked out these craft for the increasing number of recreational boaters. Today, restored boats promenade the lakes. Their sleek silhouettes of varnished mahogany, brass fittings, and leather interiors conjure up visions of the regattas of the 1920s. These valuable assets required their own buildings, and the boathouse as an essential element of camp was born.

The Stokes' boathouse on Upper St. Regis Lake, circa 1890. (Courtesy of The Adirondack Museum)

Another Adirondack Icon: The Guideboat

Early settlers in the Adirondack lake country found boats to be the most reliable transportation, and by the 1870s a swift, elegant craft had evolved. The guideboat owed its origins to working coastal watercraft like the dory and wherry, but it used naturally curved spruce roots for ribs and stems and quartersawn cedar or pine for planking. This was planed to the thinnest possible width that could still tolerate weight. Many new visitors to the region mistake these boats for canoes, but guideboats are designed to be rowed, not paddled.

In the early 1900s, boatbuilders flourished in Newcomb, Long Lake, Saranac Lake, and Old Forge, and each imparted his own unique and subtle variations, expressed in stem shape, deck details, rib spacing, overlap, and even seat construction. Guideboats were essential to a guide's livelihood — as important as a horse to a cowboy — and cost about $40 a century ago. Nowadays you'd be hard pressed to acquire a new one for less than $6,000, and fine antique boats have been appraised from upwards of $10,000. Guideboat yokes and seat backs show up as decorative motifs on camp walls, and in the grandest lodges entire boats hang from the rafters.

O. S. Phelps
Chief Guide of Survey.

Contemporary boathouses are built much the same way they were 100 years ago, with the exception of the type of lumber used. Today, for docks, decks, and floors, pressure-treated lumber replaces the rough-hewn timbers of a previous generation. For foundations, cribs filled with stone are sunk, piers are submerged, and the boathouse is integrated into this substructure. The boathouse exterior should reflect the style of the main camp. Lakeside approaches should be as intriguing as roadside entrances. Many boathouses have second floors that are often used as living quarters, a great room, or for recreational space. Sometimes their design is more "deck-like," and the flat roofs lend themselves to sunning and outdoor entertaining.

Three vintage guideboats built by: (top) H. K. Martin, circa 1915; (middle) George and Bliss Co., circa 1906; (bottom) Fred W. Rice, circa 1900. All of the boats are still in use by the owner.

▲ *Part of the Topridge complex, this is arguably the most documented boathouse in the Adirondacks. Cedar has never looked better or had more personality.*

75

◄ The Buttercup II is a replica of a boat on Long Lake. The original Buttercup was the first public steam launch on the lake in 1885. The guides in the area, sensing unwanted competition, axed the bottom of the boat and sank it. To emphasize their point they blew up the dam at the end of the lake the same night. It was ten years before another steam launch was put on the lake. The Buttercup was resurrected in 1959 by scuba divers, and it currently sits behind the town offices in Long Lake. Its namesake is an electric launch, built by Elco, which has a gold-plated engine to eliminate corrosion.

➤ The upper floor of the boathouse at The Point on Upper Saranac Lake highlights the diversity of uses for the boat garage. The interior design is an unusual combination of the romantic and the nautical.

➤ A contemporary boathouse on Raquette Lake exhibits an unusual bungalow roof and arched truss system, built by Bob Waldron. Dormer windows echo the contour of these supports.

Outbuildings

Most camps have outbuildings that hide unsightly machinery or provide an escape from the houseguests. Outbuildings are a ubiquitous element of camp: pumphouse, outhouse, doghouse, icehouse, woodshed, art studio, gazebo, teahouse — any or all of these may be part of the camp complex.

It is also impossible to discuss camps and their structures without mentioning outhouses. When nature calls, this primitive but handy shanty becomes a destination resort all its own. They come in many styles — one-holers and multiple-holers — and have even been known to be outfitted with mahogany seats!

◄ The underside of the cross gables in this teahouse create an angular skeleton that is accentuated by the elliptical barrel vault.

➤ The chapel at Camp Tapawingo. A Mohawk word, Tapawingo means House of Joy. Mac and Margo Fish purchased the property in the 1950s, when a single cabin was the only dwelling. Over the years, they have brought all of the building materials in by wheelbarrow or float and built the various camp structures by hand. Raised walkways meander from building to building. The owners have also built much of the furniture, using naturally fallen trees from the property. The camp has the aura of Swiss Family Robinson and is perfect in its imperfection.

Mac Fish is the retired chaplain of the Lawrenceville School. He built the chapel of glass and cedar for family services. It is a spiritual place: a place for music, religion, contemplation, and inspiration.

This imaginative outhouse, built by artist Bruce Gunderson, speaks of Russian log structures and the stave churches of Norway. Gunderson's work is primarily in unpeeled cedar, which is abundant in the Adirondacks.

◄ This quaint kids' bunkhouse is adjacent to the main camp and has a Japanese flavor due to the angled roof brackets. The cedar bunk beds were built by Cris Shakeshaft; the vintage bed pillows were made by Keene artist Barbara Smith.

▼ This outhouse is a miniature of the main camp.

◄ The Sod House at Topridge conceals electrical transformers and has been built around an unsightly cinder block structure. Recipe for a sod roof: put down a membrane, add dirt, roll out sod, add water.

INTERIORS

There are scattered morsels of information mentioning interior design in the early written material concerning Great Camps. Black-and-white photographs offer some clues, but use of color is difficult to discern. In William Wicks' book *Log Cabins, How to Build and Furnish Them* (1889), he illustrates a handful of items — a wood box and dining table among the most exciting. A 1912 article in *The Independent*, "Vacation Homes in the Woods" by Robert H. Van Court suggests that "a few rugs or lengths of matting may be spread upon the floors, and windows curtained with the simplest cotton prints or with plain muslin or cheese cloth." In addition, he mentions that other furnishing can include a large table for reading and writing materials, comfortable chairs with cushions, and sofas covered with blankets and "piled with cushions." This certainly wouldn't have done for Mrs. Vanderbilt, but it was and is perfectly acceptable for an unassuming camp.

Some of the architects who designed camps in the Great Camp era also designed built-in furnishings and often suites of furniture. Built-ins were embraced enthusiastically during the Arts and Crafts period (1870-1925) and many of the closet and storage areas in the camps reflected this interest. They were artfully designed as furniture-quality built-ins with compartments hidden by paneled doors. Built-in seating was evident in the form of sofas and inglenooks (benches that face each other and flank a fireplace). Wrought ironwork for fireplace and lighting was often designed by the architect as well, and made locally or, in the case of camps Kill Kare, Uncas, and Sagamore, by the blacksmith in residence. Many of the rustic accoutrements were left for the caretaker to create over the winter; the remainder was sent to the camp in crates shipped from various locations by the well-traveled owner. The matter of finishing touches and a cohesive decorating plan however, is not evident and may have been left to chance — it was an eclectic aesthetic.

In fact, travel seems to have been a major influence on what furnishings appeared at camp. With the opening of the railroad lines to the West came a new appreciation of the Native American crafts. Navajo blankets, rugs, and Pima baskets were sent back to camp. These items worked

◁ Interior designer Lauren Ostrow allowed texture to reign in this great room where minimal use of pattern lets the architecture speak for itself. The interior walls of this camp are covered in large-scale board and channel of western red cedar, which was treated with Danish oil. Michael Bird's signature diamond window is a dominant feature. He makes a concerted effort to bring light into spaces to counteract the perception of the dark camp — a request from many clients. Conceptually Bird uses two types of windows — one for viewing and one for venting — and tries not to mix functions. A large fixed-glass window is flanked by casements, thus avoiding a view eclipsed by screens.

Orientalia

Many of the original Great Camps exhibited a brazen Japanese influence, which seems an odd juxtaposition to the woods of the North Country. Consider, however, that a mania for everything Japanese had gripped the country at the beginning of the twentieth century. A previously isolated Japan had been persuaded by American Admiral Perry in the 1850s to allow American merchants in to establish trade relations.

Eventually Japan opened its doors (around 1870) to the western tourists, and tour they did. Camp owners traveled to the exotic world of the Orient or visited one of the many Japanese exhibitions held in the United States. They felt compelled to introduce Orientalia in the form of an architectural or decorative detail. This added a bit of whimsy to their vacation homes, which were taken far less seriously than their primary residences. Surprisingly, this tribute to the Orient continues in many of the new camps being built today - think of it as a reference to a reference, and it seems not at all out of place.

beautifully with the geometry of the log work, providing a primitive, earthy quality. Japanese articles appeared in the form of fans, lanterns, parasols, ceramics, and painted screens. Memorabilia from international exhibitions and journeys became trophies for display, a means of parading the owners' breadth of experience and taste.

The Arts and Crafts movement is most exemplified in the number of Mission furnishings and Craftsman-style lighting fixtures that remain in older camps. The movement was begun by William Morris in England as a backlash against Victorian excess and rampant industrialization. He campaigned for integrity in materials and craftsmanship, and went on to design furnishings aimed at creating the holistic home. His disciple in America, Gustav Stickley,

championed the aesthetic of craftsmanship and simplicity of form. He went so far as to publish a magazine, *The Craftsman*, to impress upon his minions his specific point of view. At the same time there was interest in a return to nature and, at the other end of the spectrum, a fascination with "exotic" styles and forms. This blending of various tastes and fashions was reflected in camp interiors, such as Camp Stott, with its Craftsman wall paneling, late Victorian fireplace, Indian blanket draperies, Oriental rugs, and animal trophies, or at the Inman Camp, which references Moorish arches, Japanese accessories, and American Indian patterns all in the same breath.

Today we are witnessing a return to fine craftsmanship, appreciation of nature, and things of simpler shape than seen in recent decades. Spiritually and aesthetically, this trend appeals to the mainstream, and commercially, it assumes a respectable portion of sales in the home furnishing industry. Furniture forms, lighting design, cabinetry, roof pitches in bungalow proportions, and window arrangements (large pane topped by smaller panes) have all been adopted from the Arts and Crafts lexicon. This is a home decorating movement that is compatible with the rebirth of Adirondack style; they speak the same language.

There are varying degrees of rusticity possible in Adirondack style. One could use a silk velvet ocelot print or a cotton buffalo plaid to upholster the same piece — creating an impression either of polished elegance or of a rugged cabin in the woods.

An old pack basket loaded with greens, sticks, and antlers makes an impressive table arrangement. Barn board is an excellent interior siding for a new camp. It is inherently rustic and lends character to a room lacking personality.

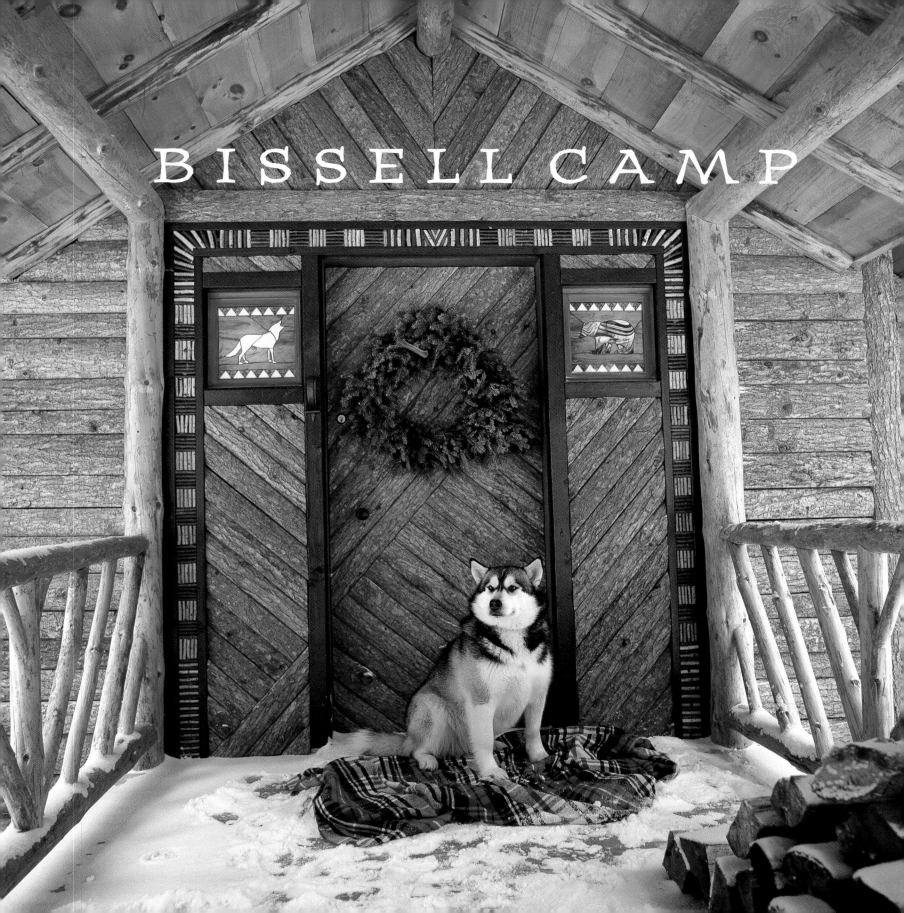

CHIP BISSELL, ADIRONDACK DESIGNER, AND HIS WIFE, SANDY, DESIGNED THIS WONDER IN THE WOODS THEMSELVES. "It wasn't so much the building of a house as it was a huge art project," Chip said. They are both artists and had always looked to the trees as inspiration for their watercolor paintings. When it came to designing their camp, they began to think of trees as potential elements in their new home.

Structural influences came from various lodges at the now-defunct Lake Placid Club, a place the couple spent their childhood summers and where they were married. Imagination and a heartfelt love of the woods have never been more visible than in this camp. The Bissells have lavished attention on every detail, down to the peeled twig doorstops.

Throughout the camp, red pine has been used for the pillars. These were first peeled, then scrubbed with hot water. They were dried and then treated with boric acid to prevent bug infestation. The worm markings evident on many of the pillars are caused by woodworms that remained under the last layer of bark, leaving a natural hieroglyphic.

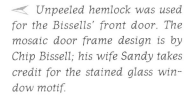

Unpeeled hemlock was used for the Bissells' front door. The mosaic door frame design is by Chip Bissell; his wife Sandy takes credit for the stained glass window motif.

An "outside-in" front vestibule dreamed up by Bissell was accomplished by continuing the roofline of the exterior walkway canopy into the great room. The hooked rug wall hanging is by Bissell's grandmother, a New York State champion skeet shooter. An oversized stuffed mayfly (honoring a popular trout fly) graces the roof of the "outside-in."

➤ This reading nook was designed to have the same square footage and calculated feel of sitting in a bathtub, a favorite place to catch up on literary pursuits. To achieve the diamond pattern, Bissell glued tar paper onto the Sheetrock and snapped chalk lines on the diagonal. Pieces of birch bark were cut into squares and applied, with twig overlays secured by Don Beaney, a twig specialist who is on builder Peter Torrance's crew.

◄ This unusual shelving was designed by Chip Bissell and made from a tamarack tree. Disks were sliced from the trunk and placed in descending order according to diameter. The vertical logs had a wedge cut so the heartwood could be removed, allowing the outer rings of the posts to shrink without splitting the outside shell. Danish oil was applied to preserve the wood and give it a warm glow.

⋎ Vowing that "There will be no taxidermy or pieces of dead animals in this home," the Bissells' challenge was to find the appropriate chandelier for the great room. The solution was a tamarack root ball that was yanked from the ground on family property. The root ball was hung to dry; the top was routed out and then electrified.

◅ *A bedroom aerie looks out over the High Peaks. Birch trees were taken from the property and used as filigree in the octagonal space. The first spring in the camp the owners were delighted by leaves that suddenly bloomed on these trees, proving that you can fool Mother Nature. The bedside lamp was made by Bissell from a portion of a tree that had grown around a wire fence.*

➤ *The Bissell guest bath displays clever use of three of the woods found on the property: a tamarack counter, white cedar stickwork, and a diminutive cherry shelf.*

⋎ *The owner selected cedar following a "blowdown" — a major windstorm — and had craftsmen place it in the stair railing so that the balusters would resemble a whale's ribcage.*

⋎ *Throughout the camp the Bissells recycled bathroom fixtures found in old homes and salvage yards. The claw foot tub was used in the master bath and "gussied up" with bandana tiebacks.*

Color and Materials

An article by Harvey Ellis in a 1903 edition of *The Craftsman* titled "The Adirondack Camp" proposes that woodwork should have no paint, and that a simple dark olive-brown stain would work on beams, casings, and doors. For the great room he called for walls washed with a dull yellow ochre in order to give a khaki appearance. He suggested that the dining room should exhibit old rose walls (instead of tawny yellow), and that bedrooms needed a cool blue gray. Throughout the camp the woodwork, except the floor, should be brown, and kitchen, offices, and utility rooms should be stained a strong grass-green. One can only imagine the horrific interior that would result from this poisonous palette.

Today's year-round camp interior must have a color palette that is pleasing in all four seasons. It requires a different combination of colors than a home in Florida, for example. The dark winter months in the far north require the use of bold color in small or large doses as an antidote to the thin gray light that prevails. Pale yellow offers feeble juxtaposition to the white ground, ashen sky, and leafless trees. Light blue is too cold. Strong colors that would be unthinkable to pair in a room anywhere else, greens and reds for example, become compatible in this part of the world. Interior wood stains should have a modicum of warmth, against which greens, reds, jet, and khaki, as well as earthier tones such as bronze, bittersweet, and moss, work well.

◁ *This cabin on Little Moose Lake once had a dropped lauan ceiling and green shag carpeting — afflictions that plague many older camps. The Winter House, owned by interior designer Barbara Collum and her husband, Thad, was originally built as the maid's quarters for the main camp, which was designed in 1919 by architect Gus Shepard and updated by contractor Mark Hannah.*

The small cabin was restored and made majestic by raising the ceiling and using knotty white pine "V"-groove boards for the walls. They remain unfinished — a beautiful way to set off the Collums' collections. Custom-made down sofas are upholstered with a combination of antique Bessarabian rugs and a forest-green baize. Every Christmas the Collums bring in a forest of potted evergreens; they are lit from underneath by can lights. The wooden deer next to the fireplace is an ancient tomb decoration.

▷ *A living room vignette at Evergreen House: texture and pattern played against barn board sets the mood. Leather, chenille, and wool plaid are grounded by a Navajo-design rug. The coffee table is made from laurel and topped with native rough-cut granite.*

This camp was built in 1904 in the southern Adirondacks. The ceiling grid work and layering of technique in this great room is engaging. The polygonal ceiling was sheathed first with 4-by-8-foot board, then overlaid with battens that didn't cover the seams, but were placed horizontally. A final layer of log work completed the ceiling. This camp is an unpretentious structure, with the exception of the effusive work of the log craftsman. Using spruce, he built balconies, arches, and bookcases with abandon. The small box on the table in the foreground is made of birch bark and porcupine quills. The Ojibwa and Mohawks did this type of work through the 1940s.

Wall Treatment

Older camps were predominantly clad in wood, especially log, or beaded board. For those in the throes of renovation, any wood left untreated has likely darkened over time from sun exposure, age, and soot. The ambitious camp owner can have it cleaned or sanded to bring the material back to its original lighter state.

Burlap, linen, and even resin-coated paper (used to ward off dampness) were sometimes used as alternatives to cover spaces above the dado. Beaverboard (known nationally as fiberboard) was first employed in the 1920s as an inexpensive means of insulation and wall cover — the precursor to Sheetrock. Battens were tacked on to cover the joints; these could be an eyesore or a clever addition. Because beaverboard tends to disintegrate over time, its cousin, Homosote "4-40" board (made of recycled paper), is used more often. It has a fine clothlike texture that marks easily, but when painted with heavy coats of oil paint and used above the dado can enliven a room with texture and applied color. It is quintessential Adirondack.

There are a host of historical references to unusual wall finishes, such as woven splint work that is similar to the backs and seats on Old Hickory furniture. It was made in flat sheets and sold by the now-defunct Indian Splint Manufacturing Company in Geneva, New York. Another wall finish was sweet grass matting, a durable, rough material first used as a floor covering and woven by Indians in the Northeast. Sadly, neither of these products is readily available today, but grass cloth, paperbacked burlap, woven rattan, leather, cork, and oxidized copper are alternatives currently on the market. An artful wall treatment at Twin Farms, a stylish Vermont inn designed by Alan Wanzenburg and the late Jed Johnson, features a troweled plaster wall with hay worked into its undulating surface. A clever approach seen at Camp Topridge is wide-plank, thick paneling that has been rough hewn and distressed: one-inch plaster chinking applied between the boards creates a horizontal pattern.

⋀ *The log cabin at Twin Farms in Barnard, Vermont. Designer Jed Johnson was brought in to turn convention on its ear by deconstructing different themes for each room or cottage, rendering them in unexpected treatments, such as this wide plaster chinking technique.* (Photograph by John Hall)

Interior Bark and Twig Work

Then there is bark. Birch trees proliferate in the Adirondacks, so this is a decorative cover that is readily available. Bark from the white birch is tougher than it appears. It has been proven to outlast other wall coverings and paint, and has a reflective quality that can brighten a space. Each sheet of bark should be stripped and flattened with a weighted board; the bark should be applied to the wall shortly thereafter so that it doesn't become brittle. The back side is sanded down and a contact adhesive applied so that it becomes like linoleum. The bark can be left in its virginal white state, although this can be rather stark next to wood paneling. Polyurethane seals it and gives a slight sheen but adds no depth of color. As an alternative, birch bark can be aged and covered with a light application of a mixture of linseed oil, mineral spirits, and golden oak stain, followed by a coat of varnish. Any dried bark applied to an interior surface is highly flammable, so this should be taken into consideration when deciding on placement — a fireplace surround is *not* an appropriate location for bark.

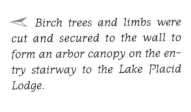

◅ *Birch trees and limbs were cut and secured to the wall to form an arbor canopy on the entry stairway to the Lake Placid Lodge.*

➤ *The yellow birch stairway in the Honeymoon Cabin at Topridge wends its way down to the sleeping quarters. The twig work is by Tom Lamb.*

Spruce and cedar bark must be soaked to be made pliable. It becomes leathery and can be used to wrap beams or as a wall covering. Another alternative is to dry the bark, and miter-cut the edges. Craftsman Don Beaney has been working with twig and bark for fifteen years and says, "There's no talent here. God has created it and we're just transplanting it."

The same twig work that is used on camp exteriors can be employed inside, and without the threat of weather, it can be rendered in a much more delicate and refined manner. In addition, there are many more alternatives for finishes on interior twig work, including staining, oiling, waxing, and painting. Restraint is in order; unfortunately, many of the new camps going up today resemble laboratories for twig experimentation and arboreal abuse rather than livable spaces.

Homeowner Eileen Griffin and interior designer Barbara Collum designed this Westport kitchen in white birch bark and twig. Craftsman Lionel Maurier has interpreted their plan flawlessly.

The master of this camp is a collector of Adirondack furniture and memorabilia, and the library was built to showcase his collections. Note the L.G.B. train in its bespoke berth. Cris Shakeshaft created the streamlined twig and log work inside and out from Eastern white cedar.

99

▲ Woodcarver Paul Stark was brought in from Oregon to put his mark on the cedar posts throughout this camp. These newel posts illustrate his depth of talent.

Flooring

In the Adirondacks, flooring for the larger spaces is always wood: 1-by-4-inch Douglas fir is an historically correct flooring, but 1-by-4-inch southern yellow pine is less expensive. Native cherry and maple also make lovely flooring. At the more esoteric end of the spectrum, architect Michael Bird prefers reclaimed antique pine floorboards in 9-to-22-inch widths. This option, however, has become prohibitively expensive as the demand has outrun the supply. Lake Placid contractor Peter Torrance favors 1-by-5-inch red birch because it's harder than cherry and has a lighter cast. In one 9,000-square-foot home, his menu of wood included: redwood board and bead walls, cherry interior doors, mahogany exterior doors, red birch and antique chestnut floors, and replaned barn board cabinetry in the kitchen, with white pine peeled pole and twig work throughout!

Slate, which comes from Granville, at the edge of the park near Vermont, is aesthetically pleasing for entry areas and hallways (especially when it has copper tones running through it). If subfloor heating is used, slate can be superb in a bath area. Other stones that are being imported to these sites, include: granite, limestone, and a variety of exotic materials from foreign sources.

◁ There are very few homes in the North Country that boast virtually no wood wall covering; this is one of them. The clean, light space is accented by a single rustic reference — birch pillars. Old shutters from a cabin were put to good use as wall decor, bringing a degree of architecture and age to the space.

Great Rooms

Great rooms are places for relaxed gathering. In the lodge formation used in camps today, the great room is just that: a room that encompasses living room, dining room, and kitchen in one predominantly open space. The focal point is the fireplace, the single most important furnishing in the camp. The sitting area surrounding the fireplace should be a welcoming place for all to gather after the day's activities. Gus Shepard made a point that a fireplace should be of "generous proportion" and should look as if it could stand without the mortar, meaning it should have tight mortar joints. The most pleasing fireplaces are ones in which the stones are not set in any identifiable pattern, but appear to have been randomly and naturally placed.

◄ *The great room at Camp Topridge is in a class of its own. Memorable for its sheer dimensions, approximately 50-by-70 feet, the room is anchored at each end by walk-in fireplaces. A massive custom-built chandelier, almost thirteen feet in diameter, is the centerpiece of the main lodge, which remains much as it was fifty years ago. Half-log construction and peeled cedar twig embellishments have aged to a warm umber; the floors of oak and inlaid mahogany have been left untouched. What has changed dramatically from the original lodge is the furnishings. The interior design firm Rogers Ford, Inc., from Dallas, has toned down all the opulent decor associated with Mrs. Post, and used texture and color to achieve a subdued elegance.*

The great room at Prospect Point, circa 1930.
(Courtesy of The Adirondack Museum)

One story recounts that when owner R. M. Hollingshead was building Minnowbrook in 1949, he instructed the stonemasons to erect a massive fireplace that had a natural appearance. He returned twice to find a fireplace that looked too citified, so he had both attempts razed. The masons were so infuriated that on the third try they literally threw the bricks and stones at the mortar — to the delight of Hollingshead who claimed their work utter perfection!

Multiple fireplaces are in vogue right now. One private camp being constructed on Tupper Lake will encompass 12,000 square feet and house nine fireplaces. Another new camp offers a fireplace in every guest room.

The Rumford fireplace, devised over 200 years ago, continues to be the best fireplace design used today. Count Rumford, an American-born expatriate inventor on a par with Benjamin Franklin, sought the formula for a well-built fireplace that would draw well, produce radiant heat, and eliminate smoke. His equation began with an interior of smooth brick, and ended with the proper relation of angles, depth and height, and slant of sides and back. Rumford discovered that shallow and high works better than deep and squatty.

The most well appointed of the new generation of camps have great rooms that feature some rustic furniture, usually in the form of tables and occasional chairs, upholstered pieces that are commodious and comfortable to the extreme, and additional case good pieces. The upholstery should have simple, straightforward lines and be covered in textural fabrics like chenille, bouclé, and herringbone; these fabrics are most appropriate historically and will withstand the rigors of camp life, as will suede and leather.

To counteract the newness of the space, recently built camps make many references to old camp in the great room — oil paintings, area rugs and blankets, taxidermy, and vintage camp ephemera — through a thoughtful mélange of old and new. The new camp owners are custodians of this legacy as well as interpreters of its future.

Massive granite boulders appear to cascade randomly around a fireplace hearth designed by Bohlin Cywinski Jackson for a camp on an Adirondack lake.
(Photograph by Karl A. Backus)

➤ *The great room at the home of Barbara and Clay Camp features antique Navajo rugs and two stone fireplaces.*

A̲ *This lodge channels the spirit of a Victorian era camp. It was designed with infinitesimal attention to the details found in older camps so that it would appear to be from an earlier generation. The owner's keen eye for decoration and the desire for a relaxed atmosphere have led to a loose translation of Victoriana — here Persian carpets lap the fringe of vintage carved Chinese rugs; paisley shawls rub shoulders with leafy prints; collections perch in the unabashed displays of a carefree connoisseur; and Oriental accents have been placed discriminatingly.*

The library (shown at right) rises two stories into a gallery, and is punctuated by a huge tarpon trophy. All of the log work, as well as the sofa table, were created by craftsman Cris Shakeshaft. The birch and twig bar was built by Tom Phillips. The project architect was Rich Hanpeter for Wareham-De Lair architects.

◁ *This great room is the hub for the spokes of Three Timbers camp. The fireplace is of natural granite from Malone, New York; the raised stone detail on its face is reminiscent of the mantels designed by Gus Shepard. The birch burl mantel was made by Tom Phillips.*

This cabin at the site of the Whiteface Inn is owned by Jon Prime, who operates the Adirondack Store and Gallery in Lake Placid and New Canaan, Connecticut. His home is a sophisticated mix of family antiques, camp memorabilia, and auction finds. A closer look at the ceiling reveals that Jon has painted the Styrofoam ceiling (that a previous owner had installed) with trompe l'oeil knots and markings to mimic birch bark.

Bluff Point, one of the early Great Camps, was built for the Frank Stott family in 1877. This great room was completed in 1888 and is attributed to W. W. Durant, Stott's son-in-law. The inscription on the mantelpiece "Mollia Tempora" (easy living/good times) is a rule strictly enforced by the current owners and their guests.

Many of the Great Camps had elaborate game rooms, either in the main lodge or in separate buildings. At this camp, a billiard room adjoins the great room. The antique leaded-glass pendant lamps cast a topaz light over the space, lending a seasoned ambience to a new camp.

Dining Areas

◄ *The Marsh Estate dining room by Centerbrook Architects. The 9-by-60-foot mural that wraps the dining room depicts the local landscape in all seasons.*
(Photograph © Norman McGrath)

Camp dining areas can be reduced to two important elements — a big table and an incredible chandelier. The scale of both should be as imposing as the space allows. At Sagamore, Mrs. Vanderbilt could seat seventy-five in her dining room. This is an extreme example of how entertaining was and still is an institution in the Adirondacks. If one oversize table takes up too much space, consider ad hoc tables and seating that can be stored until needed. Whether you entertain out-of-town guests or invite the neighbors, it's best to plan to accommodate the maximum number.

⬈ *The dining area at the Inman Camp, circa 1890.*
(Courtesy of The Adirondack Museum)

◄ The dining room at Gull Rock seats thirty-plus people and is filled much of the summer. The woman who owns this camp is an executive in the culinary industry, so dining in style is an important ingredient of each day. A collection of Arts and Crafts ceramics huddle at either end of the mantel.

➤ "Camp" doesn't necessarily mean primitive. This warm and elegant Christmas Eve dinner scene was set by Barbara Collum with her finer campware, and includes a dazzling collection of silver candlesticks, hand-painted napkins, and handblown glassware that is color-coordinated to each setting. The table is brought back to the woods with the addition of antique German lead deer, originally used for stocking stuffers, and barley-sugar deer favors placed at each setting. A set of eight American Chippendale chairs surround the table. A fireplace acts as the backdrop with an A. Osborne Mayer painting hanging over a Gus Shepard mantel salvaged from another property.

◄ The dining room at Uplands in Keene Valley is set for a ladies' luncheon. Note the wall decor — a caretaker had cut ornithological (bird) engravings from old calendars and tacked them between the studs, creating a rustic gallery. The playful addition of a string of Japanese lanterns gives the room a festival atmosphere.

◄ Barbara Collum's boathouse kitchen is set for luncheon with Lynn Chase limited-edition fish plates. Husband Thad's love of fly-fishing is apparent throughout the camp, especially in the accessories and framed art.

Ⓐ The dining area of the home of artists Paul and Lelia Matthews features hats collected for three generations. At gatherings, guests are encouraged to don a hat to break the ice.

Kitchens and Baths

The rooms of least importance to the original camp owners — the kitchen and the bathroom — have much more significance today. Consequently, there is almost no resemblance between the old and the new when discussing kitchens. In the past, the number one criteria for a camp kitchen, as Gus Shepard pronounced, was that it be "located so that prevailing winds will keep odors of cooking away from the rest of camp" and that it have a view that the servants might enjoy. Most likely it was painted in white enamel, which at least gave the appearance of cleanliness.

The new camp owners are asking more of their kitchens. Camp kitchens that are befitting a rustic home are not purchased from manufacturers' catalogs; they are either adaptations or custom-rusticated kitchens. However, kitchen cabinetry ordered from a manufacturer can be enhanced by pulls fashioned from twigs, fungi, antlers, or aged metals cast in natural shapes. Cabinet frames can be appliquéd with twig or bark for a more rustic feel, and then may be painted or varnished to protect from kitchen wear. Ideally, cabinetry should be custom built of either a rough-hewn wood or antique board. Very little can be done to disguise less attractive appliances, but with the availability of panels that can be rusticated, a more seamless transition between appliance and cabinet can be achieved. Countertop materials should have a connection with the outdoors; granite with a rough-hewn edge, soapstone, bluestone, slate, thick slabs of wood with a live edge, and even copper sheeting tacked with copper studs, are all natural elements that give the desired effect.

◄ *Excess and minimalism mingle in the kitchen of the Winter House. Craftsman Lionel Maurier from New Hampshire was brought in to build the kitchen cabinets. The appliances are beautifully camouflaged thanks to his expertise. The log cabins standing sentry-like on top of the cabinetry are antique models for camp buildings. The chandelier, designed by Barbara Collum, was made in England of red stag antlers. The table between the chairs was made by Reverend Ben Davis, circa 1930 — an unusual piece for the itinerant southern preacher, who usually worked in rhododendron root.*

⋀ *Adirondack winters are as long as ever, and offer an ideal opportunity to hunker down and make the best of it. Red La Fountaine used one winter to build this Indian Head dish rack for his cottage — a triumph of man and material over meteorology.*

➤ The La Fountaines have taken a quaint cottage and filled it with their own exuberant touches of folk art and camp. Red and Nan are exceptional cooks, and their world revolves around food and the atmosphere that accompanies it.

➤ Simplicity is taken to an art form in this spruce-lined kitchen.

➤ Echo Pond has been appended many times over the years. The new owner recently had a kitchen and dining wing added to the existing structure. The exterior stone wall with glass-block windows, from an addition in the 1950s, became the interior kitchen wall. Stone was further incorporated into the space with the introduction of the fireplace and soapstone counters from Vermont. The counters have had many coats of mineral oil applied to darken and protect them. The cabinets are of clear pine and the massive table with the "live edge" was made from oak boards framed with the logs from seven ash trees removed during excavation. The kitchen-dining addition was designed by architect Janet Mellor, the renovation and cabinetry was done by Scott McClelland, and the table was created by Dave Rogers.

Modern bathrooms, on the other hand, can be made to look very similar to their predecessors. There is an abundance of old-style sinks, tubs, plumbing, and fixtures manufactured today. Claw foot tubs, new or gleaned from salvage yards, can be found. Floor and wall tiles are available in an unbelievable assortment of basic, Victorian-style geometric tiles, as are marvelous handmade bas-relief tiles in zoological and botanical motifs specific to the North Country, such as bear, heron, squirrel, dragonfly, and pinecone. Slate and primitive-fired tiles reminiscent of Raku pottery can add a weathered quality and texture to a room of porcelain fixtures, and, as in the kitchen, twig, log, and stone treatments can produce a rustic atmosphere. Peter Torrance recently specified a hollowed-out burl for a sink in the guest bath of a home he was working on. Pebble stones set in epoxy grout can be used as a tub surround instead of tongue and groove wainscoting, and can also be installed as an alternative to tile on the shower walls — the effect can be otherworldly. Metal taps and faucets can be purchased unfinished, or the degree of gloss can be knocked down to a dulled pewter-plated or rust finish to complete the picture.

A *bathroom at the Inman Camp.*
(Courtesy of The Adirondack Museum)

◄ *An old claw foot bathtub in the Collum master bath is framed by two copper engravings from the mid-1800s struck from images of Sir Edwin Landseer paintings. Two horn fishing rod racks found in France have been cleverly employed as towel racks. The chair is a Victorian-era lead garden seat from England.*

121

An elegant camp bathroom designed by Lauren Ostrow is high-lighted by a hammered copper washbasin, granite counter, and sculptural pinecone tile mirror surround — a nature-inspired tran-quil composition.

The well-thought-out, subdued use of color is a visual accent to the exceptional design of this camp. Owner and architect referred to traditional camp materials by using milk paint colors in utility rooms as well as on floors to punch up the color and ease cleanup. The mushroom-colored chair rail mouldings capping tawny wain-scoting are a surprise.

Beaverboard is at its finest, seen above the wainscoting in the luxurious bathroom at Lean-to Camp, designed by Elizabeth Stewart. The tub deck and sink counter were specified in a fired granite with earthy copper tones.

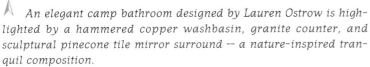

Sleeping Quarters

Camp bedrooms can be as spare as a jail cell or as elaborate as a suite in a city hotel. The bed is the focal point. Twig, bark, log, and hickory beds are natural choices. Other options range from beds in simple shapes upholstered in leather or vintage blanket patterns, to wooden bedsteads with shutter-like cutouts featuring trees, deer, and fish on headboards, and painted wood frames with rough log posts. For the artistic, possibilities include reviving a classic frame with paint, moss, and twig, or painting a rustic oil still-life on a tall Victorian headboard. Master bedrooms are a place where individual expression is encouraged. Clever camp decor in a bedroom might feature an inherited raccoon fur coverlet, a pagoda canopy, or a nautical theme.

Bunk rooms are ideal for stacking up children and conserving space. Traditional bunk beds or rows of train-like berths are an amusing interpretation. Another alternative is the sleeping porch (see following section).

◄ This fanciful master bedroom at the Collums' features a peeled maple bed with a pagoda canopy. The pattern was inspired by an early reference, from Thomas Chippendale, to Chinese twig work. The owner points out that bamboo was really the first twig furniture, and to support this theme she has brought in bamboo and rattan bed tables complete with netsukes and a magnificent antique painted screen depicting deer that she discovered in Houston.

➤ Photograph of the bedroom designed by Captain Charles Hiscoe for Kamp Kill Kare.
(Courtesy of The Adirondack Museum)

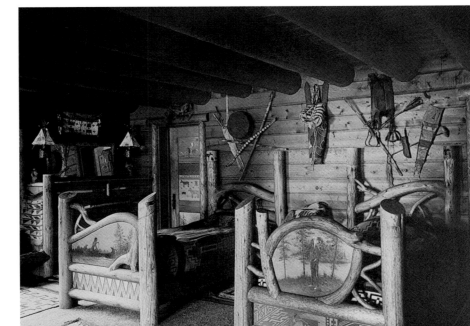

≺ Margo and Mac Fish made the canopy beds for their sleeping chamber at Tapawingo. The white textured tester throws are a rustic take on an eighteenth-century furniture form.

≻ The guest cottage of this camp was papered in birch bark by noted craftsman John Champney in 1912. The random configuration of the half-round yellow birch twigs creates a mosaic and is a rare treatment of the materials. All the rustic furnishings in the room were also made by Champney. The washstand on the left was once owned by Dr. E. L. Trudeau, the pioneer of the tuberculosis sanatorium.

≺ The one room at Cedar Rock Lodge that was not negotiable for change by husband or architect was the bunk room, designed by the owner, Helen Frenette, for her son and his overnight companions.

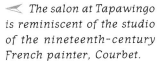 *The salon at Tapawingo is reminiscent of the studio of the nineteenth-century French painter, Courbet.*

The Treehouse Room at Twin Farms, in Barnard, Vermont. Interior design by Jed Johnson and Associates; twig ceiling scrims by Cris Shakeshaft and Dan Mack.
(Photograph by John Hall)

This cabin had been called the Bat Cave because of the vermin that inhabited it. It has been replaced by this jewel in the woods. The headboards are painted with a fall view of Lake Placid and a winter view of Whiteface Mountain. The architect was Michael Bird.

Porches

One early attraction of the Adirondacks was the presumed health-giving qualities of the air, and a significant portion of Adirondack history revolves around the work of Dr. E. L. Trudeau, who opened tuberculosis sanitoriums. He believed that with fresh mountain air, plenty of rest, healthy food, and peace and quiet, a sickly patient could be restored to full health. Trudeau built cottages for patients to "take the cure." These cottages varied in style from Queen Anne, to shingle style, to colonial revival, but one thing they had in common was the porch. Patients were required to take in the outdoors for up to eight hours a day, winter or summer, while still getting plenty of rest. Porches enabled them to do both simultaneously. Sleeping porches were built off of the bedroom so that a patient could be wheeled out to rest in the fresh air while under the protection of a roof and half-screened or glassed walls. There were open porches, glass-enclosed porches, entry porches, verandas, and sleeping porches. Some of the larger cure cottages had all of these porch types incorporated into the structure.

Soon after Saranac Lake homes sprouted numerous porches, the general public acknowledged the benefit of the outdoors, and many camps integrated the porch into their repertoire. A broad veranda became one of the most important features of the camp.

New camps feature the sleeping porch for an experience that has the essence of the outdoors, but the convenience of shelter and warmth if needed. There is nothing more enchanting than to lie on a screened sleeping porch under a blanket of stars with a late summer breeze coming through on three sides. It is like sleeping in a treehouse.

◄ A striking porch at the home of Clay and Barbara Camp at the Glenburnie Club on Lake George. Commodious red-rattan furniture with its original striped canvas was purchased from the old Saranac Inn. The modern floor lamp was painted with birch trees in mind.

◣ A Saranac Lake cure porch.
(Courtesy of The Adirondack Museum)

≪ *A pleasant mix of antique hickory, birch, and new wicker make for a serene porch setting.*

➤ *An ethereal spot for a nap, the sleeping porch at Uplands.*

➤ *This cure porch is true to the period with a spool daybed and vintage sick cart.*

Furniture

The stick and twig furniture from the woods was made by caretakers, guides, and a handful of talented craftsmen, out of imagination born from winters of solitude. Ernest Stowe, Lee Fountain, Bill Jones, and George Wilson made some of the finest examples of rustic furniture. But in the 1890s the conundrum was that camps were being built with many rooms that needed furnishing, and the caretakers and rustic furniture builders weren't able to create enough log and twig furniture to fill these spaces — nor would it have been appropriate in every room. Much of the rustic furniture built was too unrefined and uncomfortable for the inside of the house and was relegated to the porch or lawn. What was needed was production furniture that had a certain rusticity — wicker from companies such as Wakefield Rattan Co., hickory chairs and tables from Indiana, and Mission style furniture from Stickley and his competitors all seemed to work well. In addition, log and planed wood built-ins were designed by architects and builders, and upholstered with cushions. The remaining spaces were outfitted with woodsy effects. Often a camp owner would ship crates of clothing and housewares to camp, and the caretaker would use the crate to build a carcass for a chest of drawers or shelf that would be transformed with paint and twig — an early form of recycling. On some pieces, shipping information can still be deciphered on drawer sides and inside panels.

Since these were second homes, what ended up at camp was often whatever had been spurned from the primary residence, including old sofas, out-of-fashion lamps, and occasional tables. This is a tradition that is maintained today, resulting in eclectic interiors that are idiosyncratic and pure camp.

◁ *A woodland settee reminiscent of a rickshaw at Inman Camp, circa 1890.* (Courtesy of The Adirondack Museum)

Built in 1906 for Harry Levy, a beer baron from Ohio, and designed by architect Julian C. Levi from New York City, this camp is one of the few that has retained all its original furniture. The owner has acquired numerous museum-quality camp pieces over the years — more than thirty-five years ago he had the prescience to seek out camp furnishings at a time when they were underappreciated and even used for kindling. On the top floor of this boathouse is an impressive collection: a large, cedar-leg Ernest Stowe desk, circa 1906; a Daniel Vacek oil painting dated 1991; a Stowe chair circa 1906; a Fred Bass settee from Minerva, NY, circa 1915; and a Bill Jones framed print signed by the maker, from the Massawepie Childwold Park Hotel.

◅ *This applied bark and twig secretary by Ernest Stowe is on display at the Adirondack Museum.*

From the Woods

Since the late 1970s, Americans have been fascinated with folk art. We have systematically devoured each category of folk art that has been "rediscovered" — primitive weathervanes, Amish quilts, children's toys, and so on have held the gaze of the collector. The current craze for handcrafted goods, coupled with the revived interest in rustic furniture, make pieces new and old the focus of today's treasure seeker. To the beginner this style is unfamiliar and a bit eccentric, but experienced collectors will tell you that there is very little great rustic on the market, and only a handful of true artisans are able to create something Mother Nature would want to own up to. There are herds of new rustic furniture builders literally coming out of the woods, with pieces that are poorly constructed and lacking any aesthetic virtue. Additionally, the bulk of antique rustic furniture on the secondary market has been left outdoors and neglected. Consequently, bugs and rot can be problems. Look for previous repairs and loose joints due to shrunken limbs. These lessen the value of the piece, but because of the nature of the item — this is, after all, rustic — it may not be an issue. Advanced techniques in the premature aging of wood and bark have enabled new to pose as old. Only by scrutinizing enough of this type of furniture will you become an educated consumer.

Craig Gilborn, the premier authority on rustic furniture and author of the book *Adirondack Furniture and the Rustic Tradition*, divides it into categories: stick furniture, root and burl, mosaic twig, applied bark, peeled pole and branch, Black Forest, and bentwood, are among them.

Stick furniture: Just like it sounds, this style is built from sticks specifically selected for the function of the piece being built. According to Gilborn, it is then "...nailed, wedged, or tied together to form tables and seats." Some of the early work appears haphazard, although there are many pieces that are bona fide furniture. These early craftsmen did not have the classical training of a Duncan Phyfe. They used what was available to the best of their ability, and were quite proficient at their craft.

The most successful of the stick furniture craftsmen, including Ernest Stowe, Joseph Bryere, and Lee Fountain, understood their limitations and didn't aspire to a higher level of ostentatious design such as the ornate furniture from the Belter Brothers (a heavily carved Victorian style with tufted upholstery) that was popular at the turn of the century. They did experiment with forms (desks, clocks, and breakfronts) and embellishments (diamonds, stars, sunbursts, and painted scenes). Their work has lasted a hundred years and is much imitated today, down to the distinguishing details — a true testament to their talent. Pieces attributed to the pioneers of this style fetch top dollar at auctions across the continent.

Bruce Gunderson, who is noted for his intricate dioramas, created this unusual clock and titled it "Fenrisheim," after a Norse god who destroyed the world.

137

The Habitual Houseguest

These remarkable sketches and watercolors of Kamp Kill Kare near Raquette Lake were done by a gentleman named Charles Hiscoe, who was a retired English captain. It seems he was also the ever-present houseguest cum interior designer friend of Cora Woodruff, wife of lieutenant governor Timothy Woodruff. Hiscoe spent up to ten years fine-tuning the place and when the camp was sold to the Garvan family in 1914, "Hiscoe," as he signed his schematics, was bequeathed to the new owner. He aided in refurbishing the camp after a devastating fire in 1915, and often overrode the architect's design dictates (the well-known John Russell Pope).
(Drawings courtesy of The Adirondack Museum Library)

➤ Mrs. Garvan's bedroom at Kamp Kill Kare was the most avant-garde of its day, and remains the most imitated of all. Her intimidating bed with built-in bench was outdone only by the stuffed owl that perched in its upper branches. The table in the foreground is a fine example of root and burl furniture.
(Courtesy of The Adirondack Museum)

138

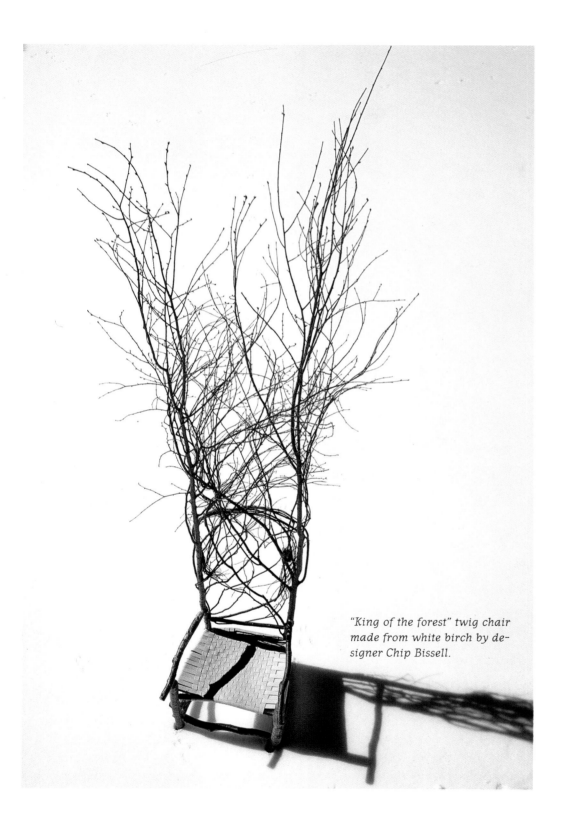

"King of the forest" twig chair made from white birch by designer Chip Bissell.

Yellow birch is considered the king of stick. It is strong and hard, and the furniture hewn from it has withstood the effects of weather and time. The bark is tight and glows with a luminescent quality not seen in other species. It is superior to white birch, which curls, peels, and flakes — a maintenance nightmare. Tom Phillips, one of the "three old men of the woods" (his comrades in bark are Barry Gregson and Ken Heitz) has been working his craft since 1985. He prefers yellow birch because of the variety in that species — its coloration can run the spectrum from off-white, to gold, to brown. He kiln-dries most of his material but has been known to use the microwave in an emergency. Occasionally he will use a green piece if flexibility is needed.

Cedar is also employed in forming stick furniture. It is bug and rot resistant and has a shaggy, textural bark. Northern white cedar has been used the most, mainly because it is found in abundance here, and it grows gnarly short limbs that are ideal for intriguing twists and curves. Cedar with birch bark design applied on the flat planes provides an excellent combination of dark and light, rough and smooth.

◄ A scene out of a snow globe: Old Hickory furniture sits patiently through the winter.

Hickory furniture falls into the category of stick built despite the fact that it is manufactured. Hickory trees do not grow in the Adirondacks, but enough of this furniture exists here that it bears explanation. At the turn of the century, literally tons of hickory furniture was brought by rail from Indiana to camps in the Adirondacks. It is a challenge to find a camp today without a piece of hickory — new or old — on the premises.

Hickory is among the hardest of American woods, the woven split-ash backs and seats give the pieces a hand-hewn quality that takes it out of the realm of factory-made. Hickory flourishes in the limestone-rich soil of Indiana and is harvested from trees that actually grow from the cut stump, and can reissue themselves up to seven times! It's hard, heavy, strong, and can be easily shaped — on this basis, an industry was born.

The Old Hickory Furniture Company in Shelbyville, Indiana, has had many incarnations. It was one of a dozen or so manufacturers of hickory furniture that sprang up in the late 1800s. Since that time the company has gone out of business, been revived, and moved to a new location. It is currently experiencing a rebirth, due to the renewed interest in nature and craftsmanship. Many of the items featured in its catalog have not changed in 100 years; they remain appealing to a new audience seeking unadorned, simple elegance.

140

Root and burl: This furniture is sometimes referred to as Gothic because of its exploitation of bizarre and grotesque shapes that form pieces with an almost medieval quality. Roots from trees and shrubs make superior bases for tables; they are sculptural in appearance and sturdy. Proper cutting of the base involves setting the root in a level pan of water and cutting at the water line. Root bases can hold conventional plank or board tabletops or can be paired with a burl top. The burl is a tumor-like growth of plant tissue that forms on trees; the most desirable are yellow birch and maple. Burls are best harvested in late fall to early spring and are then seasoned for up to two years (burl specialist Jim Howard pours on antifreeze expedite the process). Afterward, they are cut in half and coated with a mix of beeswax, linseed oil, and mineral spirits, then polished to bring out the unusual grain pattern that is characteristic of burl. They look extraordinary when the underside is routed and placed atop a root base.

▽ *A garden grotto chair made by Jerry Farrell of gnarly lilac root with an oak slab seat.*

▽ *A root table crafted by Sampson Bog Studio employs root, applied bark, and mosaic techniques of rustic furniture building.*

◄ *Detail of antiqued bark and river scene from a Sampson Bog chest.*

▽ *A cellaret (liquor cabinet) designed by architect Gus Shepard for what is now the Collums' camp.*

▽ *A slice of colossal birch burl was cleverly employed as a head- and footboard at Buttercup Lodge. It required a 4-foot chain for the saw to slice the pieces.*

Mosaic twig: This "bark-on" twig work is done with wood harvested during the winter, when bark stays put. Twigs are chosen for tone and straightness, seasoned for two to six months, cut in half lengthwise, and nailed, bark side up, onto a patterned template that has been drawn in pencil on the flat planks of wood. The designs are pure folk configurations and depict quilt-like patterns such as stars, hearts, and baskets. Many of these charmers are of mixed pedigree and combine wood from birch, cedar, cherry, red ozier dogwood, and other trees to achieve color variation.

Applied bark: A craft first worked by the Indians on canoes and shelters, this is essentially a veneer of bark applied to a piece of furniture. White birch was often used and finished with twigs that were applied to cover the seams of the veneer. Ernest Stowe, from the Upper Saranac Lake area, was the virtuoso of applied bark (see page 136); using varying tones and shapes of birch bark, he created scenes of trees and water that appeared to be painted. By reversing the bark and playing the paper white against the pinkish hue of its rind, he was able to achieve the different hues needed to portray water, land, and sky.

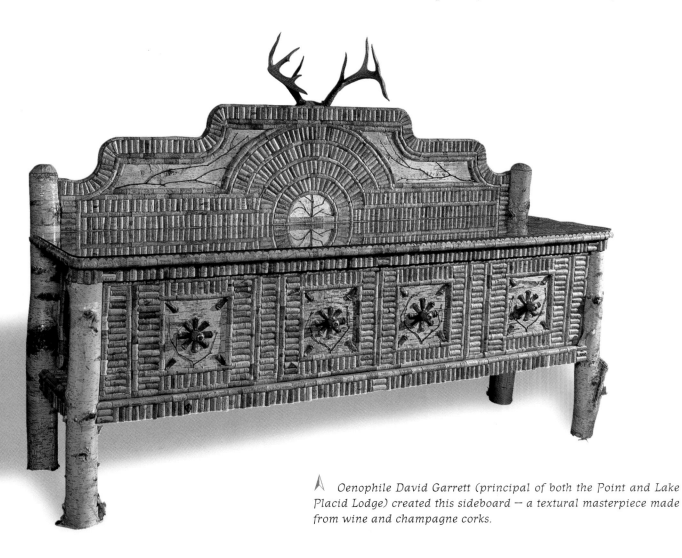

Oenophile David Garrett (principal of both the Point and Lake Placid Lodge) created this sideboard — a textural masterpiece made from wine and champagne corks.

Rustic Furniture Extraordinaire

The enormously talented Barney Bellinger began his foray into furniture only five years ago, under the name Sampson Bog Studio. Previously a sign painter and blessed with the patience and precision of a cabinetmaker, he set out on a new career. He has combined his talents to create rustic masterpieces in bark, twig, root, and stone. He was inspired by Tom Phillips, who has guided him in the technical aspects of this craft. It is a family endeavor: daughter Erin Estelle has been dotting the spots on the brook trout since she was one-and-a-half years old, and Barney's wife, Susan, paints the antique wood finishes. In the art of rustic furniture making, Sampson Bog Studio is in a class of its own.

The Sampson Bog Studio trademark.

A bark, twig, and antler hutch with a lake scene painted on the center medallion, made by Barney Bellinger.

144

➤ Cris Shakeshaft, noted twig craftsman, is seen here fitting a cedar crossbar to a desk. As a child he summered in the Adirondacks and eventually made it his home. His inspiration: the camps on Lake George. Of branch work he says it is the "slow and meticulous work ... the patient work" that appeals to him — and the stuff on which he has built a reputation.

⋀ There is a patchwork quality to the mosaic twig work of this desk, built by craftsman George Wilson around 1910.

➤ "Where the Wild Things Are": The Collums' grandchildren lay claim to this bunkroom decorated in an American Indian theme. The beds are white birch and the root table has a burl top.

145

Peeled pole and branch: Makers of this furniture use several species, including pine, spruce, and cedar. The bark is peeled, then the wood is lightly stained and finished. Without the bark, the pieces appear more like the finished furniture that Americans are accustomed to, and thus are more acceptable for interior use. They are also much easier to clean. Many pieces are made of straight log in a standard diameter, giving them a "loggy" Western look. The pieces that use smaller, gnarly branches are more intricate and more in line with what is currently being produced on this side of the Mississippi.

Black Forest: This is a misnomer. This regional folk furniture, carved with bear and foliage, is named for the Black Forest region of Bavaria. In actuality it was made in Switzerland by a family of cabinetmakers named Trauffer who continued to make this furniture into the 1950s. Linden wood was used most often because it was easy to work with; occasionally walnut was used for special commissions. The trunk of a tree was carved in the basic form of the animal and left to dry for months, at which point the detailing was chiseled in. The finished pieces were sold to tourists. Black Forest furniture found its way here as souvenirs, and recently (because of the popularity of bears in this area and the dearth and expense of genuine Black Forest creations) has been knocked-off in substitute woods from the Far East.

Bentwood: This rustic treatment is not to be confused with Michael Thonet's steam-bent furniture of the same name. Bentwood is the free-flowing weaving of branches to form a piece, where the tension of the weave holds the piece together. Much of it is made by Amish and Appalachian artisans out of willow and hickory, and has chip-carved designs that are made with a penknife.

⋏ *Peeled cedar bench with flared elephant feet from an early camp.*

⋎ *An antique Black Forest bear settee at Topridge. The pools of inlaid wood set on the entry floor are a portion of a marquetry map of the lake.*

146

△ *Adirondack chairs in a bucolic garden setting.*

▽ *Three cedar chairs built by craftsman Barry Gregson for the Lake Placid Lodge. Although these chairs are made entirely of wood, without the benefit of upholstery, the slope of the back and cup of the seat make them impressively comfortable for dining.*

Chairs of the Adirondacks

They've been seen on every other lawn and porch in North America, but the Adirondacks claim owner-ship to these consummate thrones of summer. The first Adirondack chair was designed in 1903 by Thomas Lee for his summer home in Westport, New York, hence its designation as the Westport chair. He nailed solid slabs of pine for the seat and back at a particularly pleasing angle, and added wide 4-inch arms that were ideal for set-ting a drink or book. Lee suggested to an out-of-work carpenter friend, Harry Bunnell, that he make a few of these to sell. Bunnell applied for the patent and the rest is history.

Later builders of what is commonly called the Adirondack chair had difficulty finding wide boards without knots, so they used thinner slats. There were other changes as well: backs were arched and angles were changed as each builder played with the form. The chair with a rolled seat and fanned back was born over twenty years ago when Louis Vincent of Upper Jay, New York, adapted a chair that had been brought to him for repair and dubbed it the High Peaks chair. When asked about his inspiration he merely said, "A poor craftsman is one who imitates, a good one will steal."

There are legions of manufacturers producing these types of chairs in pine, cedar, oak, and even teak. Very simply, the Adirondack chair evokes a casual lifestyle in a form that is angular, classic, and appealing.

Mission Style

This style has a dubious connection with the Spanish missions of the west and the flat-planed furniture that supposedly spawned an entire trend toward simplicity. Furniture maker Gustav Stickley popularized the movement known as Arts and Crafts in this country (despite the fact that a machine was used in the production of most of his goods). The emphasis was on function, unadorned beauty, and workmanship.

The furniture, made of quartersawn white oak, was unpretentious in design, strong, and durable. Instead of staining the oak, Stickley used an unorthodox method — he duplicated the effect of natural ammonia fumes (from animals) on barn beams, a treatment he'd seen in England. He had "fuming rooms" built with troughs filled with an ammonia solution that could alter the color of the pieces (the chairs were hung on the walls; the case goods were set on pallets). This procedure enabled him to attain a consistent finish that could not be achieved using traditional staining methods. The upholstery was of leather or sheepskin with a minimal use of ornamental appliqués in copper as the finishing touch. This style was much imitated at the time, although Stickley stayed one step ahead of the pack by branding his pieces with shop marks to protect his designs.

Mission furniture fell out of fashion by the end of World War I, but remained popular with camp owners. In his 1965 book *The Encyclopedia of Furniture*, Joseph Aronson was of the opinion that "The style lacked charm or subtlety; its clumsy weight and decorative poverty quickly condemned it and by 1913 it was extinct." A premature obituary! Since 1980, there has been a renewed interest in the Mission style. Its well-made, unadorned construction and clean lines appeal to a young, sophisticated consumer, and the Stickley company has responded by offering over 200 pieces in their current line. In response to this renewed interest in Mission furniture, there are now many independent craftsmen and other manufacturers working in the Mission style.

There is also a tremendous interest in the antique market for Mission furniture. In 1988, a sideboard owned by Gustav Stickley was auctioned at Christie's and sold for $363,000. Currently, interest is focused on pieces featuring copper inlay created by Stickley designer Harvey Ellis. A desk by Ellis recently sold for almost $60,000.

◅ Muted earth tones define this antique Mission seating area at Camp Gull Rock. Note the photograph on the dresser by Edward Curtis, the preeminent photographer of Native Americans.

Embellishments

It is an art to assemble an interior that appears casual and uncalculated while hitting the right chord of perfect imperfection. There are certain components that have been common to all camps since Durant's time; they distinguish a camp from just a home. On their own these adornments can be ordinary, but when pulled together under one roof they make a statement. Embellishments provide the final, most visible and tactile layer of color and texture to a camp—they give it identity.

A wall-hung natural demi-lune of burl from a Norway maple is supported by intricate ironwork forged by Steve Joslyn.

Wrought Iron

This black, forge-formed metal has had its place in camp since the first door was latched. There are great deposits of iron ore in the Adirondacks, and there were a number of ironworks scattered throughout the North Country. While local forges produced mostly nails and railroad parts, many of the men were capable of finer work. Into the mid-1900s towns like New Russia, Tupper Lake, and Speculator had blacksmiths who were adept at fashioning fireplace tools, lighting, and hardware to accessorize camps. Designs may have been provided by architects or by European pattern books that made their way to this country as inspiration.

The art had all but ceased until recently, because the custom work done by the nearly extinct local blacksmith lacked an audience. This may have been a blessing, as the upstart ironworkers of today are not beholden to any previous design dictate and are free to interpret in their own style. There are a number of commercial forges operating today that offer an assortment of rustically inspired wrought iron accessories and hardware ranging from door latches to drapery hardware and wall sconces. These are easily found in stores, catalogs, and through interior designers.

It was a talented blacksmith who formed these wrought iron twisted basket andirons that sit two-and-a-half feet tall. They were originally made for a camp on Doctor's Island on Upper Saranac Lake.

A procession of deer grace the headboard of this whimsical wrought iron bed. Susie Frenette of the Raquette River Quilters was commissioned to appliqué the stag and quilters' points on the duvet cover. (Photograph by Nancie Battaglia)

In the Adirondacks, naming your camp is considered a whimsical touch, not an ostentatious statement. The sign at Bearhurst is one of the many distinctive markers found throughout the area.

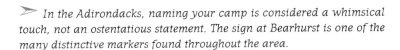

Forging a New Camp Style

Steve Joslyn, from Syracuse, New York, is a blacksmith who came to his craft through the art of jewelry making. He was struck by the variation in scale used by the blacksmith and found his own niche as a fabricator of steel, incorporating jewelry-like detail, such as the intricacy of the veins on leaves, into his work. His often elaborate pieces are forged or hammered into shape from steel bars. Major elements are left black, while details are burnished to a steel gray or brass color, and then waxed as a final finish. Commissioned pieces that have made their way across the country include lighting, fireplace accessories, and drapery hardware.

The 7-by-7-foot chandelier shown here took sixteen weeks to make. An intricate piece, it holds thirty lights.

Lighting

Most late Victorian and early twentieth century homes were lit by gas. Piping was required to reach the burner on the lamp, and lights had to aim upward as a safety measure. Many homes built during this era had a combination of gas and electric for plumbing and wiring, since it was not clear at that time which method the public would embrace. Camps featured large ceiling fixtures, found predominantly in the great room and dining room. An authentic contemporary camp should have one major chandelier, whether it be made out of antlers, wrought iron, electrified twig, or a basic wagon wheel.

In the past, utility rooms got utilitarian fixtures that were small and dim. The introduction of electricity to the home and the invention of a new, brighter bulb in 1911 freed up the design of lighting fixtures, and allowed more liberty in fashioning them. At the same time, the Craftsman style emerged. Simple square forms interpreted in copper and iron were part of the aesthetic movement and were ideal for the geometry of camp. Due to the current Craftsman revival, there are numerous companies that reproduce indoor and outdoor lighting in authentic styles and shapes (see Sources, page 175). Craftsman lamps in oak or copper, and sconces that resemble wall lanterns fit well with the austere lines of Mission-style furniture. Weathered finishes such as verdigris, brushed or hammered copper, and rust are appropriate, shiny brass is not.

A soft light is conducive to the relaxed mood of the Adirondack camp, and lamp shades are an important element in conveying this impression. Shades in art glass and mica come with Craftsman pieces, while shades of parchment, rawhide, painted oil paper, and rice paper with natural materials crafted into them work well with other camp-friendly fixtures and cut down on harsh light. For the historically correct, a reproduction carbon filament bulb that gives off one-third the light of a regular lightbulb is now available through lighting stores.

This lantern at Camp Midwood is a classic. A yellow birch bark canopy laced onto branches makes an outstanding luminaire. The original silk shade, which was shredded from heat and age, has been replaced with a parchment substitute.

Naos Forge wrought this iron chandelier featuring leaping stags for the entry at Camp Topridge.

The unusual Craftsman-style chandelier in Jon Prime's dining room was found heaped in a box at an auction and revived with some "spit and polish." The large photograph, depicting a fishing scene in Quebec, had been part of an inspirational exhibit hung by the Canadian National Railways in their terminals.

The architectural firm of Bohlin Cywinski Jackson designed the lighting and furnishings for this camp, resulting in a fully integrated project. The silhouetted trees (left) were cut from steel plates that have been allowed to rust. Fish shapes (above) were cut out as negatives in sandblasted steel reflectors that softly reflect the incandescent light.

(Photographs by Karl A. Backus)

This almost-medieval sconce at the Collum boathouse was designed by architect Gus Shepard.

Taxidermy and Wall Decor

Taxidermy is the ancient custom that became an art form three hundred years ago. It is the craft of preserving skins by stretching them over artificial body forms to represent lifelike characteristics of the living animals. Taxidermy gained prominence in this country following the Civil War, with the growing interest in natural history, museum exhibitions, and trophy hunting in Africa. It became a threat to ecological systems when entire species were being wiped out by the hunt, and soon game laws and natural park preserves were required to salvage the remaining wildlife that hadn't ended up on a wall or somebody's dinner plate.

Conservation notwithstanding, there are still many antique creatures available to enhance a camp interior. The ambitious treasure hunter can find old mounted moose, wildcat, and beaver at flea markets and auctions. Deer, bear, and fish are still abundant enough to have a hunting season, and judging from the traffic at northern shops, taxidermy remains a lucrative profession. Skins of deer, raccoon, and bear make excellent throws over sofas, on floors, as bedspreads, or hung on the wall. (A word of warning on taxidermy: the chemicals used to preserve skins have the potential to be poisonous. Therefore, it is important to keep them out of kitchen and keep handling to a minimum. The worst possible place to hang a moose head is over a fireplace, as this will surely speed its demise — but that is just where most of them end up.)

Antler accessories are a newer addition to camp decor; these were more of a Bavarian and western tradition until recently. Now, however, antler lighting, mirrors, and furniture are the current craze of the camp owner.

The first antler accessories were Gothic candle chandeliers seen in Europe around 1400. They were mounted with antlers joined by the head or torso of a carved virgin. Around 1800, horn furniture began appearing in cabinetmakers' catalogs, and by the 1850s, the Victorians had gone wild for horn furnishings. At the Crystal Palace Exhibit in London in

◁ *The fireplace at Bearhurst is one of the more extravagant, and features large cedar columns, angular capital blocks and mantel; elaborate ironwork, and a mountain lion poised on top. The ironwork was created by an Adirondack renaissance man of the early 1900s, John Buyce, from Speculator. Not only was he a proficient blacksmith, but also an excellent guideboat builder, woodworker, repairer of boats and cars, and a saddle and hardware aficionado. The sign over his shop read, "Odds and Unusual Things That You Can't Get Done At The Other Place," an understatement at best.*

▷ *This highly unusual Victorian umbrella stand from the collection at the Saranac Lake Free Library is a prime example of taxidermy gone awry.*

➤ *The spectacle of skin on display at McAlpin's trophy room at Brandreth, a privately owned preserve.*
(Courtesy of The Adirondack Museum)

1851, a German exhibit of staghorn furniture captured the fancy of huntsmen of the British Isles. In the United States, the first documented pieces of horn furniture were made by a man named Wenzel Friedrich who came to Texas from Bohemia in 1853. He worked primarily in longhorn steer and exhibited his work in expositions in various parts of the country. It really wasn't until the 1980s that antler accessories became so pervasive in the decorative ensemble of the Adirondacks; it would now be impossible to imagine camp without them.

There are many other objects that can be used to decorate camp walls. The expansive walls in these large homes require large pieces of artwork, or collections of items. There is nothing more disheartening than seeing a lone piece of art on a big wall. The common denominator for most well-appointed camps is the prominent display of one or more fine oil paintings executed in a wilderness theme and framed in an impressive old gold leaf frame.

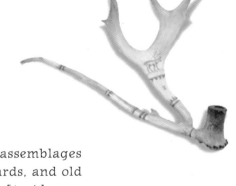

The game room at the La Fountaines' is an artsy blend of Victoriana and folk. The mural of Whiteface Inn was painted by the late Averil Conwell, a local artist, and restored by Red La Fountaine. The ceilings have been washed with blue sky and clouds as a means of opening up the space and eliminating the encumbrance of structure.

Adirondack is a style that is conducive to collections. Appropriate wall assemblages include groupings of framed ephemera such as old maps, vintage postcards, and old photographs in antique frames. For those who don't care for the implications of taxidermy, outdoorsmanship can be alluded to by hanging fly-fishing rods and mounted lures. Sporting goods from an earlier era, such as old wooden skis, rawhide snowshoes, and elegant guideboat paddles, can also work well. A single fishing rod on display can look odd, while a collection of fifteen hung on a large wall can be sublime. Thirty oars hung on an inside gable wall can be stunning. In fact, birdhouses, bird's nests, or virtually anything hung artistically in a grouping can make a handsome addition to a room. Because many of the great rooms have vaulted ceilings, the air space above the seating area is a grand opportunity to suspend a guideboat or birchbark canoe (see Stewart Camp, page 164). These are usually hung against a wall on their side so the inside rib work can be appreciated—thus providing an architectural element to an otherwise stark open space.

Fabrics, Floor Coverings, and Blankets

There is an abundance of fabric on the market today offered in designs appropriate for the camp: Navajo and kilim-inspired geometrics, fur and faux fur, wildlife fabrics depicting fish, deer, and moose, and fabrics with natural motifs such as leaves, pinecones, and berries. A small amount of the literal can work well and be a playful addition to traditional plaids, checks, nubby chenilles, prewashed twills, leather, and suedes. The selection of fabrics should appear as if accumulated over time — fight the urge to have everything match.

For window coverings linens, union cloth, and twills are good choices; lately, handsome wools in solid and plaid have caused a stir. New offerings in sheer fabrics adorned with leaves, dragonflies, and feathers are perfect for a change of pace in the summer. Many older camps had folded blankets hung by rings to form self-valances. Rods of wrought iron, oxidized copper, twig, painted wood, or even old wooden ski poles are fitting; antlers make superb tiebacks. A room should have multiple layers of texture, from the wall finish and stonework down to the pillows and curtain rods. Tactile and visual surface variations work to achieve a subliminal sense of rustication and create a tasteful balance.

Floor coverings should look like they've been in camp forever. A lightly worn Oriental rug gives the room a certain sense of dignity that a new rug can't. Layering rugs lends a carefree attitude to the composition and feels cushy underfoot. Flatwoven Navajo or kilim rugs look excellent when placed near a rug made of an animal skin. Hand hooked area rugs are superb for small spaces, and woven rags are ideal for sleeping quarters and covered porches. Sea grass mats work well on porches because they don't

The matriarch of the family had lost her patience with the small area rugs that kept guests slipping and tripping. In a fit of anger and ingenuity she tossed out the rugs and painted their replicas on the bare floor.

mildew and the dirt drops through. Miraculously, all of these rugs can be harmonious under the same roof if placed smartly. Rugs can also make a sofa look well-dressed when thrown over its shoulders; they can also serve as runners on tables, or even be used for upholstering furniture.

Whether piled high in a basket or thrown over the back of a sofa or at the foot of a bed, blankets are at home in camp, especially vintage blankets. As antique dealer Barry Friedman points out, Pendleton and Beacon have become generic names for blankets in wool and cotton. The original wool Pendleton blankets made in Oregon were created especially for the Native American market to be traded like currency. These blankets were used as articles of clothing, for gift giving, and in barter. Some are still being manufactured and remain an important part of Indian culture. The motifs and colors were inspired by the design sense of the western tribes and interpreted by the blanket mills. These blanket designs were originally limited to square patterns, but more modern Jacquard equipment was added to the looms so that many variations in design and coloration could be achieved.

Beacon blankets were of cotton and were made in New Bedford, Massachusetts. The owners of Beacon saw the success that Pendleton enjoyed by advertising to the white trade, and jumped into the market with a less expensive cotton version. These blankets were plentiful at Adirondack camps and a staple for children being sent to summer camp. With the advent of man-made fiber in the 1950s, Beacon ceased production of their ethnic and pictorial cotton blanket until a recent reissue. According to Friedman, the most sought-after Indian or camp blankets are pictorials (very rare) and primary colored wools (notably red and black). A premium is paid for cotton blankets in lavender and pastel colorations.

Trapper blankets from Canada's Hudson Bay Company and Baron Woolen Mills were used early on as a standard of exchange for beaver skins. The worth of the blanket was determined by its weight, which was indicated by the number of points (thin dark lines). For years, Woolrich has manufactured red-and-black buffalo check utility blankets that have been identified with the Adirondack mountains. The pattern and coloration of the original buffalo check has since been adapted to fabric in all scales of checks and plaids and is used often in camps. There are a plethora of blankets—horse blankets, service industry blankets made with hotel insignias, homespuns, and so on—that are perfect for camp use.

Many of the antique blanket dealers sell first-quality and "cutter" blankets. Cutters are blankets that have holes or stains and cannot be displayed in their entirety. These are ideal for upholstering headboards or cornices, or making pillows or Christmas stockings.

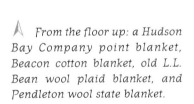

From the floor up: a Hudson Bay Company point blanket, Beacon cotton blanket, old L.L. Bean wool plaid blanket, and Pendleton wool state blanket.

Accessories

Small decorative elements count, and without them a room is a shell of what it could be. This is where most camp owners lose interest and falter, and interior spaces take on the aura of a hotel room. Although it takes time for the new homeowner to build collections, getting started is relatively easy. Buying new pieces that have been "worked over" to appear old lacks imagination, and the rooms will show it. Old leather-bound books are a venerable addition to vacant shelves and make for good reading on bad-weather days.

Collections of fungi, moss balls, birds nests, pinecones, and feathers cost only the effort it takes to forage in the woods for them. Baskets of all types that show some history make ideal receptacles for these treasures. Vintage bedding (e.g., chenille bedspreads), linens, and china can be found at flea markets and auctions. Big-league buyers may be in the market for original Frederic Remington wildlife bronzes (he spent quite a bit of time in the Adirondacks), although these can run upwards of $75,000. Those recast from the originals are more affordable, costing between two hundred and several thousand dollars. Prowling antique and flea markets can turn up sterling stags, authentic Indian artifacts, and many other camp finds, which can be introduced into the decor once the stage has been set.

The basket has its origins as a storage and work vessel used by many of the eastern tribes, notably the Mohawk and Abenaki Indians. Many of the baskets seen in museum collections display splints woven with dyed moose hair and porcupine quill. In the 1860s the fancy basket came into being. These were woven by the Indians as decorative accessories and then marketed to the general public. In a Quebec Indian community called Pierreville, on the south side of the St. Lawrence River, entire families were involved in basketmaking. In 1922, it was estimated that this town produced over $250,000 worth of baskets. The families brought their baskets and birchbark canoes to the Adirondack resort areas during the summers and sold to the tourist trade from the back of their trucks.

Ash is used today as it was hundreds of years ago. It is stripped, pounded, and soaked until it is pliable enough to weave. Strips are woven to produce the most common of basket forms — the pack basket. With their web or leather straps, which are used to hold the basket in place on the back, they remain great carryalls for hiking and wonderful containers for an elaborate arrangement of natural greens and grasses, or a simple collection

Black Forest-style bears and a collection of fungi gathered on mountain hikes help create the ideal setting for a winter's repast at Echo Pond. The china is a pattern from the defunct Lake Placid Club.

162

Three examples of Syracuse China: (left) Bisby Lake Collection; (center) Sagamore Lodge Plate designed for Mrs. A. G. Vanderbilt, bordered in 23K gold; (right) Moss Lake Collection.
(Courtesy of Collection: Syracuse China Archives)

Dining in Style

In 1880, the Onondaga Pottery Company, a pioneer in the field of ceramics, began producing vitrified china, which is produced by firing under extremely high temperatures, and is a stronger grade of china than bone china. Using clay and other regional components, the product was called Syracuse China. The company began its foray into hotel ware in 1897. Much research went into designs for shapes, decals, and glazes, making them a front-runner in the area of commercial china. Because of this, and its proximity to the Adirondack Park, the Onondaga Pottery Company produced dinnerware for hotel and camp alike. The plates shown are from private camps and hotels whose designs and logos were developed by the company. In 1966, Onondaga Pottery was renamed for its most renowned product — Syracuse China.

of walking sticks placed by a door. The older the basket the better, in terms of display. The same can be said for the fishing creel, a basket with a strap that is used by anglers to hold the fish they've caught. Both pack and creel grouped together on a mantel and filled with mosses, stones, and greens can dress up an otherwise bland space.

An unlikely but popular collectible is the lowly bracket fungus. Also known as "poor man's canvas," it has been the blank slate on which many inspired visitors have showcased their artistic talents. These fungi can be etched, carved, and painted, and are often used like a woodland diary to document meaningful camp happenings, such as climbing a peak, winning a race, or other events. This art has been in practice for centuries. Once the fungus has been dislodged from the tree it should be etched or carved with a sharp-pointed tool within a few days before the fleshy skin dries out. Experts advise the best time to harvest fungus is in the late fall, since, once etched, it will display more color variation.

Other collectibles with a history in the Adirondacks include balsam pillows popular since the 1880s, and vintage weird wood souvenirs, the heavily lacquered ash novelties popular in the mid-twentieth century.

The Adirondack Museum antiques show is held each September and features the finest assemblage of rustic antiques in the country. It is one-stop shopping for camp owners looking to outfit their place with camp ephemera. Shown here is the Christiby's booth.

STEWART CAMP

MANHATTAN ARCHITECTURAL AND INTERIOR DESIGNER ELIZABETH STEWART IS AS ELOQUENT IN DESCRIBING HER PROJECTS AS SHE IS IN ARTICULATING THE DRAWN DETAILS. She designed this camp for her family in 1986 to continue the family tradition of vacationing in the High Peaks. Stewart sought to honor the rustic ethic by selecting simple materials, and worked closely with contractor Peter Torrance and architect Robert Bradbury, Jr. to achieve a home that would be an extension of her family's love for the mountains, as well as a practical place to maintain. There is a synergy here of architecture, interior design, and feng shui. The result is a fine example of holistic design expressed in the camp vernacular.

Classic elements have been employed to tweak rustic. Stewart wanted the floors to have the well-worn look of a barn. The floors were laid in an overscaled pattern known as *parquet de Versailles*, and secured with large hand-wrought iron nails. Workers then brought in wheelbarrows of rocky dirt and scrubbed it into the 12-inch rough pine floorboards. Still not satisfied with the effect, Stewart had motor oil rubbed into the floors, inadvertently creating a disastrous sludge. Fortunately the contractor produced a chemical cleanser to clean up the oily goo and, voila, Stewart had "truly" rustic barn floors.

Surface treatments were important; the kitchen ceiling has planking set in a herringbone pattern—a classic take on an early southwestern architectural reference. In the sleeping quarters, a traditional dado design was laid out in 4-by-8-foot panels. The walls above the dado were either covered in beaverboard that was washed with a lively color, or upholstered in fabric to add pattern and soundproof the space.

◄ *The Stewarts' great room is a study in scale. Because of the size and verticality of the space, Elizabeth specified the substantial 2-inch-wide, weathered rough pine planking to be laid horizontally for the walls. The specific articulation of the cantilevered balcony brought scale to the room. Stewart is without peer in her layering of pattern and color, giving this space interest and depth of character.*

◄ The Rumford principle was pushed to the limits in the dimension of this granite fireplace. The Stewarts use a French rotisserie/andiron setup when entertaining, and can cook for thirty in this fireplace. The room required refinement, and the windows presented the opportunity to introduce it. They found a local cabinet and window maker to create the six 9-foot panels, beautiful French doors, and Gothic clerestory windows. A double veneer of mullions was used to ensure the energy efficiency of the glass. This well-traveled couple has furnished their camp with finery and flea market finds from around the globe.

➤ The stairway gallery at the Stewarts. Elizabeth laughs at the "gallery" reference, "It is what it is!" which is a clever placement of naive and local old paintings, photographs, and posters.

Will Stewart collects sepia-tone photographs and has judiciously hung them under the watchful gaze of the deer in the entry hall.

Camp Guide

Here are resources to help you experience the
atmosphere and style of the Adirondacks firsthand,
whether you choose to visit the area
or just peruse the list of architects, builders,
interior designers, manufacturers,
craftspeople, and retail stores that
feature camp merchandise.

THE GREAT CAMPS

Some of the original Great Camps are gone or have been radically changed by man and nature. Howard Kirschenbaum, founder of Adirondack Architectural Heritage, a regional nonprofit historic-preservation organization, has compiled a list of Great Camps. This list includes many from Kaiser's inventory and a few additions.

According to Kirschenbaum, a Great Camp should be a single-family estate built of rustic materials in an artistic design set on a lakeshore. There should be multiple buildings, and the camp must be self-sufficient. The following is a compilation of camps past and present.

Bearhurst, *Lake Pleasant*: built in 1894 for Herman Meyrowitz, the optical magnate.

Bluff Point, *Raquette Lake* (originally CAMP STOTT): built in 1877 for Frank Stott, a textile manufacturer.

Bull Point, *Upper Saranac Lake*: designed by architect William Coulter, built in 1899 for financier Otto Kahn.

Camp Carolina, *Lake Placid*: designed by architect Max Westhoff, and built in 1913 for Caesar Cone, textile mill owner.

Camp Cedars, *Raquette Lake*: built in 1880 for Frederick Durant (cousin of William).

Camp Cobblestone, *Spitfire Lake*: built for the daughters of George Earle Jr.

Debar Park, *town of Duane*: built around 1900 for Robert Schroeder, a German brewer. Rebuilt in 1939 for Arthur Wheeler.

Duryea Camp, *Blue Mountain Lake* (now the summer resort, **The Hedges**): built in 1880 for Col. Hiram Duryea, an industrialist.

Eagle Island, *Upper Saranac Lake*: built by William Coulter in 1899 for Levi P. Morton, former U.S. vice president and governor of New York.

Eagle Nest, *Eagle Lake*: built in 1935 by architect William Distin for Walter Hochschild.

Echo Camp, *Raquette Lake*: built in 1883 for Phineas C. Lounsbury, governor of Connecticut.

Camp Fairview, *Raquette Lake*: built in 1879 for C. W. Durant Jr.

Inman Camp, *Raquette Lake*: built in the 1890s for Horace Inman, a box manufacturer.

Camp Katia, *Upper St. Regis Lake*: begun in 1890 for George E. Earle.

Kamp Kill Kare, *Lake Kora*: begun by W. W. Durant in 1898 for Timothy Woodruff, lieutenant governor; renovated for the Garvan family in 1915 by architect John Russell Pope, following a fire.

Kildare Club, *near Tupper Lake*: designed by architects Scopes and Feustman; the current complex, finished in 1906, was originally owned by railroad magnate William Seward Webb.

Knollwood Club, *Lower Saranac Lake*: designed by William Coulter, built in 1899 for the families of Louis Marshall, Daniel Guggenheim, Elias Ashiel, George Blumenthal, Abram N. Stein, and Max Nathan.

Litchfield Chateau, *near Tupper Lake*: designed by New York architect Donn Barber; building completed in 1913 for Edward Litchfield, a lawyer/land developer.

Longwood, *Upper St. Regis Lake*: begun in 1906 for George Brewster.

Markham Point Camp, *Upper Saranac Lake*: built in the early 1900s for Dr. Samuel Baldwin Ward.

Meigs Camp, *Big Wolf Lake*: begun in 1916 for Ferris Meigs, owner of the Santa Clara Lumber Company.

Minnowbrook, *Blue Mountain Lake*: designed in 1949 by William Distin for R. M. Hollingshead, a wax manufacturer.

Moss Ledge, *Upper Saranac Lake*: built in 1898 for Isabel Ballantine.

Nehasane, *Lake Lila*: designed by architect Robert H. Robertson, and begun in 1893 for William Seward Webb.

North Point, *Raquette Lake*: built for James TenEyck; sold to Mrs. Andrew Carnegie in 1902.

Camp Pinebrook, *Upper Saranac Lake*: designed by William Coulter and built in 1898 for Levi P. Morton.

Camp Pine Knot, *Raquette Lake*: begun in 1876 by W. W. Durant; the last building was erected in 1900 for Collis P. Huntington.

Pine Tree Point, *Upper St. Regis Lake*: originally built for H. M. Twombly; reconstructed by Japanese workmen in 1902 for the Frederick Vanderbilt family.

Prospect Point, *Upper Saranac Lake*: designed by William Coulter and built 1903-04 for financier Adolph Lewisohn.

Read Camp, *Little Simon Pond*: designed by the New York architectural firm Davis McGrath and Shepard; finished in 1906 for William A. Read.

Sagamore Lodge, *near Raquette Lake*: built in 1896 by W. W. Durant and sold to Alfred G. Vanderbilt in 1901.

Camp Santanoni, *near Newcomb*: designed by Robert H. Robertson of New York; begun in 1888 for Albany banker Robert C. Pruyn.

Sekon Lodge, *Upper Saranac Lake*: designed by William Coulter for financier Isaac Seligman (exact date unknown).

Stokes Camp, *Upper St. Regis Lake*: building begun in 1883 for the Stokes family.

Camp Topridge, *St. Regis Lakes area*: first buildings put up in 1897; in 1920 cereal heiress Marjorie Merriweather Post converted this into a complex with builder Ben Muncil.

Camp Uncas, *Raquette Lake*: built in 1890 by W. W. Durant and sold to J. P. Morgan in 1896.

Wellscroft Lodge, *Upper Jay*: built in 1900 for lumber heiress Mrs. Wallace C. Smith.

Wenonah Lodge, *Upper Saranac Lake*: built in 1915 for Julius Bache, financier.

White Pine Camp, *Osgood Pond*: designed by architect William Massarene; built in 1907 for Archibald White; became the summer White House for President Calvin Coolidge in 1926.

Camp Wild Air, *Upper St. Regis Lake*: original buildings designed by the owners' niece and built in 1882; subsequent buildings designed by architects McKim, Mead and White for Whitelaw Reid, publisher of the *New York Herald Tribune*.

Camp Wonundra, *Upper Saranac Lake* (now the hotel, **The Point**): designed by William Distin and built during the years 1930 to 1933 for William Rockefeller.

Glimpsing the Great Camps

Many Great Camps are located on private lakes at the end of very long private roads, so getting a very close look is out of the question. However, there are entertaining ways to see and even experience firsthand a half-dozen or so of these remarkable places.

Great Camp Sagamore, located about four miles from the village of Raquette Lake, is open for guided tours from May through October. Visitors can see the main lodge, the Wigwam, the dining building, some of the sleeping cottages, and the fine service complex. Sagamore also sponsors numerous workshops and Elderhostel sessions. There are also "Great Camp" weekends that take you to see other Raquette Lake-area sites (Uncas and Pine Knot, among others) that are rarely open to the public. Call (315) 354-5311 for a schedule.

White Pine Camp, on Osgood Pond, near Paul Smiths, was Calvin Coolidge's summer White House in 1926. Although it's not strictly rustic in the details, the complex does fit the Great Camp mold, with a string of woodsy cottages along a quiet lakeshore, boathouses, a lovely Japanese teahouse on a peninsula, and spacious buildings for dining and recreation. White Pine is open for tours from spring through fall, and cottages are available to rent by the week during the summer. Call (518) 327-3030.

Camp Santanoni, on Newcomb Lake, is abandoned, but its access trail makes an excellent cross-country ski or mountain bike trek (ten miles round trip). The route passes the farm that supplied milk, eggs, and meat for the Pruyn family a hundred years ago. Recent repairs have stabilized the structures, and in summer months architectural history interns give talks on the site. It's also possible to get to Santanoni by hiring a horse and wagon; check in Newcomb for a list of outfitters.

The dinner-and-cruise boat **William West Durant** offers an excellent narrated tour of Raquette Lake from May through October, passing Echo Camp, Pine Knot, Bluff Point, North Point, and other lovingly preserved Great Camps. Trips are by reservation only. Call (315) 354-5532 for a schedule.

The organization **Adirondack Architectural Heritage** sponsors lectures across the park and tours of Great Camps designed by William Coulter during the summer. Early reservations are a must. Call (518) 834-9328.

The Adirondack Museum has the one remaining building from Camp Cedars on its campus, and an extensive collection of fine rustic furniture in a large rustic summer home. In early September, the Rustic Furniture Fair features some forty builders from across the country. The museum's education department offers occasional field trips to Great Camps led by architectural scholars. Call (518) 352-7311.

For the self-motivated, a canoe can be a great way to see Great Camps from the water. While there's no "star map" for locating these places, paddling around the St. Regis Lakes, Upper Saranac Lake, and Raquette Lake gives you a view of exteriors. These lakes all have public boat launches or public beaches where you can put in, but please respect the private property and don't set foot on dock or shore. On Upper Saranac Lake for example, you can glimpse Wenonah Lodge, Sekon Lodge, Levi Morton's camp on Eagle Island (now a Girl Scout camp), and Lewisohn's Prospect Point, now a Christian summer camp.

SELECTED BIBLIOGRAPHY

Aronson, Joseph. *The Encyclopedia of Furniture*. New York: Crown Publishers, Inc., 1965.

Bond, Hallie E. *Boats and Boating in the Adirondacks*. Blue Mountain Lake, New York: Adirondack Museum/Syracuse University Press, 1995.

Calloway, Stephen and Cromley, Elizabeth. *The Elements of Style*. New York: Simon and Schuster, 1991.

De Sormo, Maitland D. *The Heydays of the Adirondacks*. Saranac Lake, New York: Adirondack Yesteryears, Inc., 1974.

Dix, William Frederick. "Summer Life in Luxurious Adirondack Camps." *The Independent*, July, 1903.

Donaldson, Alfred L. *A History of the Adirondacks*. New York: The Century Company, 1921. (reprinted Fleischmanns, NY: Purple Mountain Press, 1992)

Ellis, Harvey. "An Adirondack Camp." *The Craftsman*, July, 1903.

Gallos, Philip L. *Cure Cottages of Saranac Lake*. Saranac Lake, New York: Historic Saranac Lake, 1985.

Gilborn, Craig. *Adirondack Furniture and the Rustic Tradition*. New York: Harry N. Abrams, Inc., 1987

Gilborn, Craig. "Oh For a Lodge in Some Vast Wilderness." *Victorian Society of America: Nineteenth Century Magazine*, Summer, 1976.

Gilborn, Craig. *Durant, The Fortunes and Woodland Camps of a Family in the Adirondacks*. Sylvan Beach, New York: North Country Books, 1981.

Gilborn, Craig. "The Westport Chair." *Adirondack Life* (May/June 1982).

Hild, Nancy. "The Right Angle." *Adirondack Life* (July/August 1989).

Hotaling, Mary B. "Paint Colors in Adirondacks Architecture." *Adirondack Architectural Heritage Newsletter*, (Fall 1996)

Hotaling, Mary B. "Ben Muncil, Master Builder." *Adirondack Architectural Heritage Newsletter*, (June 1997).

Hotaling, Mary B. "Framing A Legacy." *Adirondack Life*, (March/April 1997).

Jamieson, Paul. *The Adirondack Reader*. Adirondack Mountain Club, 1982.

Johnson, Krissa. "Tree Houses." *Adirondack Life*, (January/February 1986).

Kaiser, Harvey H. *Great Camps of the Adirondacks*. Lincoln, Massachusetts: David R. Godine, 1982.

Kirschenbaum, Howard. "Endangered Architecture." *Adirondack Life*, (September/October 1985).

Kirschenbaum, Howard. "Thirty-four or More?" *Adirondack Life*, (May/June 1985).

LaBastille, Ann with Newton, Beulah. "Adirondack Mailboats." *Adirondack Life*, (Summer 1974).

Lee, Nancy. "Putnam Camp." *Adirondack Life*, (November/December 1980).

Malo, Paul. "A Home to Call Our Own." *Adirondack Life*, (November/December 1997).

McMartin, Barbara. *The Great Forest of the Adirondacks*. Utica, New York: North Country Books, 1994.

Murray, Reverend William Henry Harrison. *Adventures in the Wilderness; or Camp Life in the Adirondacks*. Boston: Fields, Osgood, and Company, 1869.

Newman, Bruce. *Fantasy Furniture*. New York: Rizzoli, 1989.

Nutting, Wallace. *New York Beautiful*. Garden City, New York: Garden City Publishing Co., 1936.

Orton, Vrest. *The Forgotten Art of Building a Good Fireplace*. Dublin, New Hampshire: Yankee Books, 1969.

Schermerhorn, C.E. "Adirondack Cabin, an Ideal Summer Home." *Beautiful Homes Magazine*, date n/a. Early 1900s.

Shepard, Augustus D. *Camps in the Woods*. New York: Architectural Book Publishing Co., Inc., 1931.

Taussig-Lux, Karen. "Diamonds in the Rough." *Adirondack Life*, (November/December 1995).

Van Court, Robert H. "Vacation Homes in the Woods." *The Independent*, June, 1912.

Way, Daniel. "Nature's Canvas." *Adirondack Life*, (September/October 1985).

Wicks, William S. *Log Cabins: How to Build and Furnish Them*. New York: Forest and Stream Publishing Company, 1889.

Williams, Donald R. "Souvenirs of Wild Wood." *Adirondack Life*, (September/October 1995).

SOURCES

ANTIQUES

Black Bass Antiques
Lake Shore Drive
Bolton Landing, NY 12814
518-644-2389

Correll Antiques
499 North Main Street
Gloversville, NY 12078
518-725-7310

Linda Davidson
296 Lakeshore Drive
Berkley Lake, GA 30096
770-448-2773

Laura Fisher Antiques, Quilts, and Americana
(blankets and rugs)
1050 Second Avenue
Gallery #84
New York, NY 10022
212-838-2596

Barry Friedman
(Navajo blankets and rugs)
P.O. Box 55492
Valencia, CA 91355
661-255-2365

Kelter Malce
74 Jane Street
New York, NY 10014
212-675-7380

Lake Placid Antiques Center
105 Main St.
Lake Placid, NY 12946
518-523-3913

Magoun Bros.
125 Ryerson Hill Road
South Paris, ME 04281
207-743-2040

Moose America
P.O. Box 7
Rangely, ME 04970
207-864-3699

Greg Peacock/Log Cabin Antiques
86 Main Street
Lake Placid, NY 12946
518-523-3047

Alan Pereske
Saranac Avenue
Lake Placid, NY 12946
518-891-3733 (for appointment)

Reflections
7 Main Street
Lake Placid, NY 12946
518-523-8115

Burt Savage/Larch Lodge
Route 126, Box 11
Center Strafford, NH 03815
603-269-7411

With Pipe and Book
(old books, etchings, maps, and postcards)
91 Main Street
Lake Placid, NY 12946
518-523-9096

ANTLER ACCESSORIES

Crystal Farms
18 Antelope Road
Redstone, CO 81623
303-963-2350

Charlie Jessie
250 McKenzie Pond Road
Saranac Lake, NY 12983
518-891-5383

Tom Welch
The Rustic Homestead
P.O. Box 68
Minerva, NY 12851
877-251-4038

ARCHITECTS/ ARCHITECTURAL DESIGNERS

Michael Bird, A.I.A.
77 Riverside Drive
Saranac Lake, NY 12983
518-891-5224

Bohlin Cywinski Jackson
182 North Franklin Street
Wilkes-Barre, PA 18701
570-825-8756

Robert Bradbury, Jr., Architect
873 River Road
Piermont, NY 10968
914-359-1373

Camens Architectural Group
126 West Main Street
Malone, NY 12953
518-483-1585

Carrington/Meyers Design Studio
201 Sheperd Street
Raleigh, NC 27607
919-829-9929

Centerbrook Architects and Planners, LLC
Box 955
Centerbrook, CT 06409
860-767-0175

Crawford and Stearns Architects and Preservation Planners
134 Walton Street
Syracuse, NY 13202
315-471-2162

Richard Giegengack, A.I.A.
2901 Q Street NW
Washington, DC 20007
202-338-9531

Rich Hanpeter, A.I.A.
38 Main Street, P.O. Box 32
Saranac Lake, NY 12983
518-891-2815

Jed Johnson and Associates, Inc.
211 West 61st Street, Suite 502
New York, NY 10023
212-489-7840

Nils E. Luderowski, A.I.A.
Route 73, P.O. Box 52
Keene Valley, NY 12943
518-576-4446

Janet Mellor, Architect
354 Averyville Road
Lake Placid, NY 12946
518-523-4641

Elizabeth Stewart Design
12 East 86th Street, Suite 809
New York, NY 10028
212-737-1964

Stracher-Roth-Gilmore, Architects
143 Jay Street
Schenectady, NY 12305
518-374-9412

Wareham-De Lair, Architects
71 Bloomingdale Avenue
Saranac Lake, NY 12983
518-891-2360

BUILDERS

Bob Becker
260 Park Street
Tupper Lake, NY 12986
518-359-3932

Steve Blakely
62 Hyland Drive
Lake Luzerne, NY 12846
518-696-3986

Steve Dubrovsky
151 West Shore Road
P.O. Box 338
Bethel, NY 12720
845-583-6500

Baird Edmonds
Route 73
Keene Valley, NY 12943
518-576-4401

Mark Hannah
P.O. Box 895
Old Forge, NY 13420
315-369-3979

Terry Hanrahan
P.O. Box 171
Lake Placid, NY 12946
518-523-9840

Jack Levitt Construction
19 Birch Street
Lake Placid, NY 12946
518-523-3273

Scott McClelland
Hurricane Road, P.O. Box 554
Keene, NY 12942
518-576-2008

Peter Moles (with Ken Johnson)
Lake Placid Club
Lake Placid, NY 12946
518-523-1625

Schoolhouse Renovations
5 High Street
Tupper Lake, NY 12986
518-359- 9141

Guy Schweizer
Route 186, P.O. Box 19
Lake Clear, NY 12945
518-891-3392

Chris Tissot
30 Shepard Avenue
Saranac Lake, NY 12983
518-891-2278

Peter Torrance
Cascade Road
Lake Placid, NY 12946
518-523- 3225

Bob Waldron
Box 502, Route 28
Raquette Lake, NY 13436
315-354-5787

Craftspeople

Adirondack Stained Glass Works
29 West Fulton Street
Gloversville, NY 12078
518-725-0387

John Bryan, Artist in Wood
198 Milliken Road
North Yarmouth, ME 04097
207-829-6447

Barbara Smith
(vintage fabrics and pillows)
Glen Road
Jay, NY 12941
518-946-7625

Kip Trienens (stained glass)
Pleasant Street
Westport, NY 13997
518-962-4801

Interior Designers

Barbara Collum Decoration and Design
6976 Colonial Drive
Fayetteville, NY 13066
315-446-4739

Diamond Baratta Design, Inc.
270 Lafayette Street
New York, NY 10012
212-966-8892

Johnson-Wanzenberg and Associates
211 West 61st Street, Suite 502
New York, NY 10023
212-489-7840

Moose Creek Ltd.
1592 Central Avenue
Albany, NY 12205
518-869-0049
also
10 State Route 149
Lake George, NY 12845
518-745-7340

Ann O'Leary/Evergreen House Interiors, Inc.
71 Main Street
Lake Placid, NY 12946
518-523-4263

Lauren Ostrow Interior Design, Inc.
30 Park Avenue
New York, NY 10016
212-532-6999

Rogers-Ford Inc.
2616 Thomas Avenue
Dallas TX 75204
214-871-9388

Iron and Metalwork

Naos Forge
1817 East Avenue Q, Suite C15
Palmdale, CA 93550
661-273-5851

Steve Joslyn
1244 State Highway 80
Smyrna, NY 13464
800-985-9811

Trainbrook Forest
HCR1 Box 18
Paul Smiths, NY 12970
518-327-3747

Wild West Designs
Pete Fillerup
P.O. Box 286
Heber, UT 84032
435-654-4151

Lighting

Arroyo Craftsman Lighting
4509 Little John Street
Baldwin Park, CA 91706
626-960-9411

Brass Light Gallery
131 South First Street
Milwaukee, WI 53204
414-271-8300

Bill Epps
1134 Military Parkway
Mesquite, TX 75149
972-285-1004

Living Light at Lean-2 Studio
P.O. Box 222
Adirondack, NY 12808
518-494-5185

Rejuvenation Lamp and Fixture Co. (mail order)
2550 N.W. Nicolai Street
Portland, OR 97210
888-401-1900

Timeworks Unlimited
P.O. Box 9052
College Station, TX 77842
979-690-1368

Rustic Furniture Builders

Adirondack Rustics Gallery
Route 9
Schroon Lake, NY 12870
518-532-0020

Glenn Bauer
RR1, Box 77
Vermontville, NY 12989
518-891-6933

Barney Bellinger Sampson Bog Studio
171 Paradise Point
Mayfield, NY 12117
518-661-6563

Jerry Farrell
P.O. Box 255
Sidney Center, NY 13839
607-369-4916

Eric Glesmann
9732 Starr Hill Road
Remson, NY 13438
315-831-5339

Bruce Gunderson
P.O. Box 97
Keene, NY 12942
518-576-2015

Hawkins Unique Rustic and Mosaic Art Furnishings
4621 Markey Road
Roscommon, MI 48653
517-821-6985

Ken Heitz
Box 161, Route 28
Indian Lake, NY 12842
518-251-3327

Jerry's Wood Shop
(Adirondack chairs)
Box 116, Route 30
Speculator, NY 12164
800-548-5041

Dan Mack
14 Welling Avenue
Warwick, NY 10990
845-986-7293

Lionel Maurier
26 Tucker Mountain Road
Meredith, NH 03253
603-279-4320

Nick Nickerson
P.O. Box 618
Copake, NY 12516
518-329-1664

Old Hickory Furniture Co., Inc.
403 South Noble Street
Shelbyville, IN 46176
800-232-2275

Tom Phillips
Bartlett Carry Road
Tupper Lake, NY 12986
518-359-9648

David Robinson
515 Tuxford Court
Trenton, NJ 08638
609-737-8996

Crispin Shakeshaft
2427 Route 9 N
Crown Point, NY 12928
518-597-3304

L. and J. G. Stickley, Inc.
Stickley Drive, P.O. Box 480
Manlius, NY 13104
315-682-5500

Jamie Sutliffe
Cold River Woodworks
Long Lake, NY 13679
518-624-3581

Stores Specializing in Adirondack

Adirondack Arts and Crafts
104-106 Main Street
Lake Placid, NY 12946
518-523-4545

Adirondack Country Store
252 North Main Street
Northville, NY 12134
800-566-6235

Adirondack Store and Gallery
109 Saranac Avenue
Lake Placid, NY 12946
518-523-2646
also
90 Main Street
New Canaan, CT 06840
203-972-0221

Eddie Bauer Home
(mail order)
P.O. Box 182639
Columbus, OH 43218
800-426-8020

The Birch Store
Route 73
Keene Valley, NY 12943
518-576-4561

George Jaques
Box 545 Main Street
Keene Valley, NY 12943
518-576-2214

Tiger Mountain Woodworks — The Summer House
2089 Dillard Road
Highlands, NC 28741
828-526-5577

Whispering Pines
(mail order)
43 Ruane Street
Fairfield, CT 06430
800-836-4662

Taxidermists

North Country Taxidermy
Route 73
Keene, NY 12942
518-576-4318

Smith's Taxidermy
15 Broadway
Saranac Lake, NY 12983
518-891-6289

Lodging

The following is a selective list of places to stay in the Adirondacks. The accommodations range from cabins with shared baths to rooms with granite Jacuzzis. All are guaranteed to leave the guest with a lasting impression of the Adirondacks, and a desire to return.

The Adirondack Book: A Complete Guide (Berkshire House, 2000) is the authoritative travel guide to the region, listing lodgings, restaurants, museums, cultural attractions, shops, and other useful information.

Bearhurst Cottages
South Shore Road
Speculator, NY 12164
518-548-6427

Covewood
Big Moose Lake
Eagle Bay, NY 13331
315-357-3041

Elk Lake Lodge
Blue Ridge Road, P.O. Box 59
North Hudson, NY 12855
518-532-7616

Friends Lake Inn
963 Friends Lake Road
518-494-4751

The Hedges
Off Route 28, P.O. Box 209
Blue Mountain Lake, NY 12812
518-352-7325

Hemlock Hall
Maple Lodge Road, P.O. Box 110
Blue Mountain Lake, NY 12812
518-352-7706

Highwinds Inn
Bartons Mine Road
North River, NY 12856
518-251-3760

Lake Placid Lodge
Whiteface Inn Road
Lake Placid, NY 12946
518-523-2700

The Mirror Lake Inn
5 Mirror Lake Drive
Lake Placid, NY 12946
518-523-2544

Northbrook Lodge
Off Route 86
Paul Smiths, NY 12970
518-327-3379

The Point
Upper Saranac Lake
Saranac Lake, NY 12983
518- 891-5674

Timberlock
Indian Lake, P.O. Box 1052
Sabael, NY 12864
518-648-5494

The Wawbeek Resort and Restaurant
553 Panther Mountain Road
Tupper Lake, NY 12986
518-359-2656

CREDITS

PHOTOGRAPHY

All color photographs by Gary R. Hall unless otherwise indicated. Photograph on page 1 © 1998 by Carl E. Heilman II.

page 8 *Autumn on Lake George.* Lithograph by Currier & Ives. Courtesy of a private collector.

page 11 Early Dutch map of Canada and New England. Courtesy of a private collector.

page 12 *American Forest Home.* Lithograph by Currier & Ives. Courtesy of a private collector.

page 14 (top) Antique postcard. Courtesy of a private collector; (bottom) Photograph by Stanley Harris. Courtesy of *Adirondack Life* magazine.

pages 16 & 18 Postcards © Dean Color, Glens Falls, NY.

page 74 *O. S. Phelps, Chief Guide of Survey.* Courtesy of The Adirondack Museum.

page 84 Photograph by Katherine McClellan. Courtesy of Smith College Archives, Northampton, MA.

page 169 Red Maple, Tamarack, and White Pine leaves. Lithograph courtesy of a private collector.

pages 170–71 (background) *Mount Haystack from Upper Ausable Inlet,* drawn by Verplanck Colvin, from the *Seventh Report of the Adirondack Survey,* 1880. Courtesy of a private collector.

pages 179–80 (background) Ice boating; (left) Skijoring. Courtesy of the *Lake Placid News;* (right) Ski class in the early 1920s; and (left) a skit at the Lake Placid Club circa 1950s, courtesy of Ruth Prime. (left) Saranac Lake Winter Carnival, 1911, courtesy of the Adirondack Collection, Saranac Lake Free Library.

ACCESSORIES

page 2 PILLOWS on sofa, *Churchill Weavers,* P.O. Box 30, Berea, KY 40403; CERAMIC POTS, *Potluck Studios,* 23 Main St., Accord, NY 12404.

page 30 (bottom) PLACEMATS, *Chateau X,* NY, NY; NAPKIN RINGS, *Island Birch,* 1200 Wildhurst, Trail Mound, MN 55364; FLATWARE, *Vance Kitira,* 245 Fourth St., Passaic, NJ 07055.

page 44 BOWL, *Potluck Studios,* Accord, NY 12404.

page 51 TERRA COTTA POTS, *Weathered Moss Pots/Source International,* P.O. Box 4347, Blaine, WA 98231.

page 53 EVERGREENS AND DOOR ARRANGEMENT, *Adirondack Design* Ingrid Ormsby, P.O. Box 533, Lake Placid, NY 12946; CASHMERE AND FAUX FUR THROW, *Patrick Frey at The Galleries,* 225 Fifth Ave., NY, NY 10010; CHAIR, *The Great Divide,* 13 Gooseberry St., Jay, NY 12941.

page 81 (top) LITTLE BUG PILLOWS, *Chandler Four Corners,* 1 Tennis Way, Dorset, VT 05253; PILLOWS on beds, *B.B. Smith,* Box 1, Keene NY 12942; BED LINENS, *Eddie Bauer Home.*

page 82 VASE, *Country Originals, Inc.,* 3844 W. Northside Dr., Jackson, MS 39209.

page 85 All available from *Evergreen House Interiors, Inc.,* 71 Main St., Lake Placid, NY 12946; except EVERGREENS, *Adirondack Design,* Lake Placid, NY 12946; and BOW, *Baranzelli,* NY, NY.

page 91 PAINTED LURE DETAIL, *Parmalee Tolkan,* Riverside Rd., Lake Placid, NY, 12946.

page 92 EVERGREENS, *Asplin Tree Farm,* RFD 1 Box 169A, Saranac Lake, NY 12983; BLANKET, *Eddie Bauer Home;* PILLOW SHAMS AND PLANT STAND, *Evergreen House Interiors, Inc.,* Lake Placid, NY 12946.

page 93 All available from *Evergreen House Interiors, Inc.,* Lake Placid, NY 12946; except PACK BASKET, *Lake Placid Antique Center,* 105 Main St., Lake Placid, NY 12946; BIRCH CANOES, *Adirondack Store and Gallery,* Lake Placid, NY 12946.

page 99 INDIAN BLANKET on chaise, *Laura Fisher Antiques, Quilts, and Americana,* 1050 Second Ave., NY, NY 10022. PAINTED LURE DETAIL, *Parmalee Tolkan,* Riverside Rd., Lake Placid, NY 12946.

page 106 PILLOWS, WOOD CANDLESTICKS, AND PRINTS, *Evergreen House Interiors, Inc.,* Lake Placid, NY 12946; RUG THROW on sofa, *Foreign Accents,* 2825-E Broadbent Pkwy. NE, Albuquerque, NM 87107.

page 112 (bottom) VASES, *Potluck Studios,* Accord, NY 12404; NAPKIN RINGS, *Log Cabin Antiques,* 86 Main St., Lake Placid, NY 12946.

page 113 STOCKINGS, *Matt Camron,* 2702 Sackett Rd., Houston, TX 77098; NAPKINS, *Liz Wain,* 230 Fifth Ave., NY, NY 10010; BARLEY SUGAR DEER, *Dorothy Timberlake Candies,* HC 63 Box 140, Madison, NH 03849.

page 115 BLUE VASE, *The G.S. Collection,* 22 Hillcrest Ave., Lake Placid, NY 12946.

page 118 (top) WINE COOLER AND SMALL CANDLES, *Rowe Pottery Works, Inc.,* 404 England St., Cambridge, WI 53523; TABLE COVER, *Gobelin Tapestry* from Westgate, 1000 Fountain Pkwy., Grand Prairie, TX 75050; GLASSWARE, *Tastesetters,* 225 Fifth Ave. Suite 123, NY, NY 10010; NAPKINS, *Necessities,* 230 Fifth Ave., NY, NY 10010; NAPKIN RINGS, *Chateau X,* 250 Mercer St. #C602, NY, NY 10012; PILLOWS, *Baranzelli Home,* 1127 Second Ave., NY, NY 10022; HICKORY BENCH AND ANTLER CANDELABRA, *Adirondack Store and Gallery,* 109 Saranac Ave., Lake Placid, NY 12946; BOWL WITH PEARS, *Europaeus USA, Inc.,* 8 John Walsh Blvd., Peekskill, NY 10566.

page 119 TABLECLOTH AND VASE, *The G.S. Collection,* Lake Placid, NY.

page 124 BED LINENS AND PAJAMAS, *Angel Zimick,* 376 State St., Brooklyn, NY 11217; CHENILLE THROW, *Textillery,* P.O. Box 3190, Bloomington, IN 47402.

page 132 (top) PILLOWS, *B.B. Smith,* Keene, NY 12942; (bottom) PILLOWS, *Evergreen House Interiors, Inc.,* Lake Placid, NY.

page 133 PILLOWS, *B.B. Smith,* Keene, NY 12942; VINTAGE LUGGAGE, *Evergreen House Interiors, Inc.,* Lake Placid, NY.

page 145 (bottom) NAVAJO BLANKETS, *Faribault Woolen Mill Co.,* 1500 Second Ave. NW, Faribault, MN 55021; STRIPED BLANKET, *Baron Woolen Mills,* P.O. Box 340, Brigham City, UT 84302; PILLOWS on beds, *Double D Home,* shown at Details, 8701 World Trade Center, Dallas TX 75342-0163.

page 146 PAINTED LURE DETAIL, *Parmalee Tolkan,* Riverside Rd., Lake Placid, NY.

page 159 ANTLER PIPE, *With Pipe and Book,* 91 Main St., Lake Placid, NY.

page 161 BLANKETS, *courtesy of Jim Tolkan.*

page 162 BEARS, *Dr. Livingston I Presume,* 1502 E. Irving Blvd., Irving TX 75060; FABRIC, *Pommes de Pins* from Clarence House, 211 East 58th St., NY, NY 10022; DINNERWARE AND PINE CONES, *Adirondack Store and Gallery,* Lake Placid, NY 12946; TUREEN, *Cassis and Co.* at Richard Cohen Inc., 225 Fifth Ave., NY, NY 10010.

CAMP ATTITUDE

There are distinctions to be made between the native, local, and occasional residents of the Adirondacks. To have reached the exalted status of native, you must have been born somewhere inside the Blue Line, whereas a local merely has to have lived here for a couple of years, and the occasional resident need only pay taxes to enjoy his or her title. This pecking order comes with varying degrees of attitude. Natives and locals are an independent lot bordering on the obstinate. They enjoy their space and the freedom that comes with it. Likewise, occasional residents seek refuge from the metropolitan rat race and have found sanctuary in the woods. They are equally autonomous, but perhaps not as vocal as their year-round counterparts. Regardless of residential status, all are passionate about the Adirondacks. Lifetimes of memories have been made here, with some of the most breathtaking scenery in the country as the backdrop.

Maybe it's the air, maybe it's the altitude, but all who come to this area would agree that there is something particularly intoxicating about these mountains. Many Adirondack visitors show a tendency to become transformed upon their arrival; liberated from suits and schedules, they can be unaware or uncaring of any breach in decorum.

178

"Keep your temper no one else wants it."

An entertaining evening at "The Shanty," as Putnam camp was called in the late 1800s, sums it up. Dr. Edward Waldo Emerson (son of Ralph) was foraging through the garbage heap while other guests were hiking. He pulled together a suit of armor out of the cans, dishes, and sundry refuse. When the campers sat down for dinner that evening, there on the wall hung a collage of rubbish in the personification of Sir Guy Witherington Fitch-Bowditch Shantum, 6th Baron Shantum, 3rd Viscount Putnay — Emerson's creation. Further accessories were cobbled together by the diners, and a poem was dedicated to the fictitious knight.

Boisterous behavior is alive and well. A weekend visitor at a camp in Keene Valley first regaled us with his song "Don't Pick on My Pekingese," an ode to the hostess's nippy dog, and then rolled into his tongue-in-cheek version of "Down In Keene Valley." One of our hosts greeted us with a blast from his bagpipes as we entered his domain, another was exhausted from the previous night's bluegrass theme party for one hundred. These were small reminders that the traditions of camp continue more than 100 years after they were begun — both in the material form of rustic architecture, and in the intangible essence of camp spirit.

INDEX